THE WISDOM ANTHOLOGY OF NORTH AMERICAN BUDDHIST POETRY

PUBLISHER'S ACKNOWLEDGMENT

THE PUBLISHER GRATEFULLY ACKNOWLEDGES the generous help of the Hershey Family Foundation in sponsoring the printing of this book.

THE WISDOM ANTHOLOGY OF NORTH AMERICAN BUDDHIST POETRY

EDITED BY

ANDREW SCHELLING

Wisdom Publications • Boston

Wisdom Publications
199 Elm Street
Somerville, MA 02144 USA
www.wisdompubs.org

Library of Congress Cataloging-in-Publication Data
The Wisdom anthology of North American Buddhist poetry / edited by Andrew Schelling.— 1st ed.
p. cm.
Includes bibliographical references.
ISBN 0-86171-392-3 (pbk. : alk. paper)
1. Buddhist poetry, American. I. Schelling, Andrew.
PS595.B83W57 2005
811.008'0382943—dc22
2004031061

ISBN 0-86171-392-3
First Edition
09 08 07 06 05
5 4 3 2 1

Cover design by Rick Snizik

Interior design by Gopa&Ted2, Inc. Set in Minion 10.5/14.

Cover painting: "Cosmic View" by Roberta Pyx Sutherland;
courtesy of the artist.

Wisdom Publications' books are printed on acid-free paper and meet the guidelines for permanence and durability set by the Committee on Production Guidelines for Book Longevity of the Council on Library Resources.

Printed in United States of America.

CONTENTS

PREFACE

THE THOUGHT OF COMPILING an anthology of American poetry influenced by Buddhism or steeped in Buddhist lore came to me over twenty years ago. It was a compelling coincidence, and a delight that felt decades in the making, when Josh Bartok of Wisdom Publications phoned me with the concept for this book. When I had originally begun the project of searching out Buddhist-inflected poetry, I scampered about in search of poems, but never quite managed to see the shape of such a book. I never quite abandoned the idea though. From what I was reading in those days—the early 1980s—the major drawback seemed to be that only a single generation of poets had written into their books poetry that resulted from adherence to Buddhist ideas. These were of course poets who had emerged in the post–World War II era, mostly the Beats. But I wondered if in our cities and towns, or tucked back in forests or mountains, other poets were being drawn to the practices and texts of Buddhism.

Much has occurred since those months when I first imagined a Buddhist collection of North American poetry. There occurred a landmark event in May, 1987, which one day will get properly written into the annals of Buddhism, and come to be seen as one of the legendary gatherings that gave impetus to a specifically American form of Buddhist thought. Zoketsu Norman Fischer, a practice director at Green Gulch Farms Zen Center (about forty minutes by car up the winding coastal highway from San Francisco) put together a weekend retreat at which poets could talk to one another about meditation and poetry. He called the Green Gulch gathering "The Poetics of Emptiness," and opened it to the public. The Bay Area poetry newsletter and calendar *Poetry Flash* ran preliminary statements by some of the guests who had been invited to join the conference, and an attentive group turned out at Green Gulch.

Over that weekend a collection of nine writers—some of them urban-based experimental writers, some representative of rural or backwoods poetry styles, others with no particular affiliation to a school or scene—meditated together, ate together, and spent the days and evenings thinking and talking about Buddhist practice and the discipline of writing poems. Most of the poets were California residents. A run of generations was represented, from elder poets born in the 1920s and '30s to a number born in the mid-'50s. The weekend concluded with a Sunday evening performance of word, song, gong, bell, musical instruments, and wooden clappers in Green Gulch's meditation hall, a cavernous and drafty former barn. From the tree-lined carp pond out back a sangha of frogs added their voices.

In 1991, four years after that watershed Green Gulch event, Shambhala Publications released *Beneath a Single Moon: Buddhism in Contemporary American Poetry,* edited by Kent Johnson and Craig Paulenich. The Shambhala collection brought to sight a delightfully rag-tag group of forty-five poets, ranging farther than anyone might have been able to guess a decade earlier. With a preface by renowned poet and long-time Zen practitioner Gary Snyder, the book includes statements or essays by many of the contributors. This anthology was the first account of Buddhist influence on North American poetry, and as such remains a foundational volume. When it appeared Allen Ginsberg and John Cage were alive; their presence (along with Snyder's articulate preface) gave a seasoned, respectable, almost authoritative face to the book. One can't overstate the impact Ginsberg and Cage had on bringing Buddhist practice and thought into authentic discussions of modern poetry. Their influence compelled not only poets but academic critics and book reviewers to recognize Buddhist ideas as central to American poetry. In his later years, Ginsberg (who died in 1997) would tell students that Buddhism was now an indispensable point of literary reference. You simply could not discuss American literature without knowing something about meditation.

For years the poets associated with Buddhism in the minds of critics and of the larger reading public were the Beats: Ginsberg, Snyder, Jack Kerouac, Philip Whalen, Lew Welch, Diane di Prima, and their colleagues. It was easy for East Coast literary establishment figures to put down Buddhism, especially Zen, as anti-intellectual, pretentious, or as underground, reactive and romantic, and to dismiss it. By now, though, in 2005, it has become exuberantly clear that Buddhist thought and imagery are not some literary decoration dropped into poems and novels by the Kerouac generation—a "morning mushroom" (as they used to say in classical China) that fades in bright daylight and has vanished by noon.

Showing how far into mainstream culture, even pop culture, Buddhism reaches (remember, for many Americans that's all Buddhism is, a manifestation of pop culture) an anthology edited by Gary Gach appeared in 1997, *What Book!? Buddha Poems from Beat to Hiphop.* On its back cover Jane Hirshfield catches the volume's spirit. "This is no book—more a block party, complete with street bands, strolling jugglers, food you can hold in your hand and eat while walking and watching Asian-born Buddhists, American Buddhists, fellow-travelling Buddhists, honorary Buddhists, all sharing the good gossip of what can be found within practice-shaped words." Gach's collection maintains that jostling, exotic, street-market quality from the moment you break its front cover until you come out the other end. It offers a lot of material meant to stretch the definition of poetry. There is calligraphy, snippets of Dharma-combat dialogue with Zen teachers, pop-song lyrics, lectures broken into verse on the page, off-the-cuff haiku, and poems by distant fellow travelers, some of them not even particularly friendly towards Buddhism.

Now is a propitious moment for another collection to appear. It is less than ten years since *What Book?!* arrived, but suddenly Buddhism, Daoism, yoga, martial arts, and other practices from Asia seem naturalized to this continent. Grocery stores sell *Tricycle, Shambhala Sun, Buddhadharma, Yoga Journal* and similar periodicals. But I'm also thinking of the emergence of a generation of young poets who have come to Buddhism not as something exotic, rather as a tradition they grew up with. These include young Asian-American poets, and writers from across the continent for whom the retreat center is a normal alternative or adjunct to the college lecture hall.

The Wisdom Anthology of North American Buddhist Poetry is a gathering of contemporary, living poets, and contains recent work, much of which appears in book format here for the first time. Some of it is the mature work of long-seasoned practitioners, some the opening work of young writers just now publishing their first books. Think of it this way: This anthology contains work of the holders of the poetry lineages in North American Buddhism.

The notion of lineage is central to Buddhism. What teachers one has studied with, and who their teachers were, often gets traced in elaborate genealogical charts back to Shakyamuni Buddha. In certain ceremonies the entire 2,500 year succession gets chanted aloud. The Zen teacher Kobun Otokawa Roshi used to also speak in his quiet, elliptical way, of what he termed the "lost lineages." I think a quick survey of the poets associated with Buddhist teachings for 2,500 years—from India to China, Tibet, Korea, Japan, Cambodia, Europe, and the Americas—suggests that poets collectively comprise a tangle of unnamed but deeply influential lineages.

The contributors to this book, some born as recently as the 1970s, are practitioners of Buddhism, or people who have grown up readily familiar with Buddhist thought (as well as Hindu, Taoist, Confucian, Shinto, and Bön-po ideas). A few are ordained teachers in particular schools of Buddhism. Significantly, all regard Buddhism as completely ordinary—a cultural and spiritual fact of life on the North American continent.

I expect the readership of this book to include, among others, Buddhist practitioners who have not read deeply into contemporary poetry and may be unfamiliar with many of the twists and turns of thought that give rise to our poems. The introduction that follows ranges across historical forms of Buddhist poetry from Asia, its magical language, its spiritual phrasings, and looks at how poets today are working in similar modes. I expect this book's audience will also include readers familiar with the poetry of our day and on our continent, yet who may not have studied Buddhist thought in detail. These readers enter through another gate. For them too I thought it useful to focus on how the impulse of North American poetry comes into alignment with two and a half millennia of Buddhist literature—especially the writings that arose in India, China, Tibet, and Japan. Particularly now that so many writers from those cultures have appeared—and continue to come forth—in accurate translations of high literary merit.

The history of how Buddhist ideas, practices, and teachers arrived on this continent of high desert, extensive forest, and sweeping grassland, of blue jay, coyote, and Douglas fir, is documented by Rick Fields in *How the Swans Came to the Lake: A Narrative History of Buddhism in America.* He tells the stories with accuracy and riveting good humor. I'll also suggest a collection of poetry that recently appeared—*America Zen: A Gathering of Poets.* Its co-editors Larry Smith and Ray MacNiece provide a lively and informed survey of what poets practiced in Zen thought are doing.

What hasn't yet appeared is any kind of survey of the range of Asian poetries, or the poetry of the Buddhist civilizations of history, with even a cursory look at what North Americans have drawn from these traditions, in all their magical, wise, humorous, and mysterious proliferation of forms. There are indeed ways in which American poetry, doing new things in new languages, achieves the old effect of provoking spiritual insight through the art of poetry. In my introduction I draw some discernible lines of influence—and map fields of correspondence—between contemporary poets and that ongoing, archaic, sometimes thunderous, often delicate and refined, heritage from Asia. A heritage that has given us what noted scholar, poet, translator, and critic Eliot Weinberger terms "a paradise of texts."

I limited the number of poets in this book to under thirty. This way each could, in a reasonably priced volume, receive enough pages to show in detail what they are up to. I ask you to approach the collection with an open and loosely alert mind. An array of poets and readers appears here in unique configuration. This gathering—which includes you who are holding this book—will disperse after you put this book down. We will never meet under these circumstances again. An old Sanskrit verse puts it this way—

Two bits of driftwood
might meet on the great ocean

Having touched they shall drift apart
The encounters of all creatures are like this

This seems to be one teaching of the ancient buddhas, and all Buddhist traditions consider the encounter of human beings a particularly precious opportunity. If mountains and valleys reveal the bones of the ancient buddhas, rivers their veins, mist and clouds their living breath, then poetry is the voice in which they sing, chant, mewl, sigh, growl, yelp, joke, and philosophize.

There is an old Zen phrase from the tea ceremony: *Ichi go, ichi e.* "One chance, one meeting," or "this moment, just now." At this moment women and men walk among us who take to poetry with the Dharma eyes of Basho and Tu Fu, Milarepa and Ono no Komachi. Now is the opportunity to see through their eyelashes.

INTRODUCTION

THOUGH NO ONE has written the definitive 2500-year history of Buddhist literature, we do know that poetry circulated among Buddhist communities from the earliest days. The original North Indian students of Shakyamuni Buddha are well represented in the *Theragatha* and *Therigatha,* two collections of verse that were orally composed, committed to memory, and passed along through recitation or song for several hundred years before finally being written down. The songs of those first Buddhists contain vivid imagery, wildness, pathos, and enough troubled, earnest expression to provide a sharp picture of the first poets of Buddhism, many of whom must have been singers or speakers of verse before joining the order of Buddha's early followers. It is our good fortune that some of the songs associated with them were considered canonical, got written down in Pali around 80 B.C.E., and made it through the millennia to us at the outset of the twenty-first century. We can only speculate how much poetry got lost along the way or left out of the canon, and did not make it through.

The *thera* and *theri* (both words mean elder) were the wandering disciples of Buddha, male and female respectively. The word *gatha*, which refers to their songs, was a sort of catch-all term for any formal, metrical piece of verse known to the elder Buddhist order. The songs and poems circulating among the members of the order included ballad-like narratives of the poets' troubled, unsteady early lives, and accounts of their first contact with the sweet tones of the Dharma, the teachings of Buddhism. Other poems carry exhilarating tales of conversion to the Buddhist way, usually after the poet has suffered some calamitous loss of family or clan. Some gatha are brief cries for spiritual freedom, and some relate supernatural stories that give vivid coloring to how the singer achieved insight. All of the elders' songs are reliably attributed to specific individuals. Anthropologically, the poems carry precise details about Northern India in the fifth century B.C.E.

The poems of the *Theragatha* and *Therigatha* have not had a thunderous effect on contemporary American writers though. The reason is simple: The translations into English, until quite recently, have not been effective as poetry. What few translations had been done were undertaken by Sanskrit and Pali scholars during British rule of India, and the type of verse the poems got translated into is not much fun for contemporary ears. Their dull convoluted language, Victorian-era inversions, and florid phrasings were meant to plump out a Tennysonian meter. The same poor quality translations held back appreciation of classical Sanskrit poetry, which flourished during the spread of Buddhism under the Gupta Empire (ca. 350–650 C.E.). Sanskrit poetry, delicate, teeming with erotic humor, and carefully calibrated to South Asia's cultures and landscapes, has only begun to appear in commendable translation during the past twenty years. The poets W.S. Merwin, Jane Hirshfield, myself, and recently Chase Twichell, along with the late Barbara Miller (a fine scholar with an ear for poetry), have begun to bring classical Indian poetry to North America.

But the Buddhist orders of India produced other literature too, much of it passed along orally for centuries, and contemporary poets have paid close attention. Also known as gatha (though entirely anonymous), these word-artifacts include a wildly inventive range of formal language items, most of them composed in metrical verse patterns for magical purposes or to make them easy to memorize. These range from brief instructional aphorisms, goads to meditation, ceremonial chants, mealtime prayers, and benedictions, to the sort of uncrackable kernels of language that serve as magic spells and spiritual formulae (later formalized into mantra and dharani).

Among contemporary poets the influence of these types of verse is most observable when you turn to the use of meaningless or non-sensical (call them *magical*) linguistic techniques brought to bear on poetry. Here you can find the use of spells and chants built on seed syllables, or phrases of psycho-spiritual power meant to conjure (or instill) non-ordinary states of mind. Other possible directions influenced by religious or mystical texts include the direct violation of syntax and grammar. In these gestures, language is put forth not to tell stories or convey information but to render the mind susceptible to a supernatural or spiritual effect. Modern poems, like their archaic prototypes—spells, curses, fertility songs, prayers—might call a deity or supernatural guardian into manifestation, or propel a yoga practitioner or contemplative (even an unsuspecting reader) into a non-ordinary state of mind. Ezra Pound wrote that poetry "instructs, moves and delights." Here I would take the word *moves* in its most literal sense: Poetry actually carries or transports you. The next question is *where*, and that's a tricky one.

Contemporary poetry so often gets charged with being difficult; this may be because the reader expects something (a story, moral instruction, insight into character, or a direct report of information, for instance) that may not be the poet's intention at all. Keeping the magical and spiritual powers of language in mind is important when approaching any poetry, archaic or modern. With avant-garde writing in particular, you need to look for a psycho-physical effect as often as a specified meaning that could be translated into another set of words. Does it occur to readers made angry or light-headed by strange poetic techniques that they have been deliberately carried into a different state of existence? Moved into another space? (Gertrude Stein said of her critics: "My sentences do get under their skin.")

Among the early forms of Buddhist spoken-word artifacts that come close to recognizable strategies of strangeness in modern poetry are mantra and dharani. Both sorts of spells—chanted aloud, often repeatedly—are strings of sound, made potent by spiritual guides, and used by seekers to protect the mind or to carry one to specific realms of experience. Like poetry they place the qualities of sound at least as high, and usually above, any semantic content that can be extracted from them. Mantras tend to include words with recognizable meaning (the *mani padme* of the well-known mantra *om mani padme hum* means in essence "the jewel in the lotus"), but these are generally surrounded by magical syllables that have no dictionary definition (*Om* and *hum*). Dharani are little spells that have no recognizable words at all.

The linguist and India scholar Murray B. Emeneau has written something about Hindu practice that holds equally for Buddhism:

> It is noteworthy and perhaps to be interpreted as a general tendency in Hindu culture to raise certain aspects of the subliminal to consciousness, that Hinduism in general and the Tantric

> sects in particular make extensive use in ritual and religious practice generally, not only of the intrinsically meaningless gestures (of the dance and iconography), but also of intrinsically meaningless vocables. For example, the famous *om* and *hum* and the not so famous *hrim, hram, phat,* and many others, are meaningless religious noises in origin, whatever meanings are given to them by the developed dogma.

A belief many times documented among archaic or tribal traditions holds that hidden forces—deities, animal powers, protective spirits—can be called up through sounds made by the human voice. These beings lie coiled within the articulations and percussive noises of speech—the compressive thrust and friction of consonants, the vibrations of semi-vowels, the hot hissing of sibilants, the cool tonal opening of vowels. Surely this connection between voice and unseen powers goes back to the origins of speech during the last Ice Age. Spirit language, ancestral language, animal language, the playful speech of children, the nonsense expressions of lovers—all focus on the subliminal powers of sound to move us.

Poets have always known and worked these possibilities. Poems use a thousand techniques to achieve insight, or to explore realms of mind that rational thought cannot visit, maybe can't even imagine. Sometimes writers can be obdurate that, in the words of Archibald MacLeish, "A poem should not mean but be." And William Carlos Williams wrote "A new world is only a new mind."

Most of the strategies of poetry (I call them the poet's toolkit) tend in this direction. Repetition and variation of sound and phrase. The metrical dance of syllables upon the page, or along the breath. Echo, half-echo, and near-echo, everything called rhyme. Then suddenly—that fierce leap of excitement the heart experiences when ordinary words come into abrupt, unfamiliar alignment: an unpredictable thought has been born in your breast. Hoa Nguyen, who appears in this anthology, writes poems that use unfamiliar juxtapositions of words to create tender surprising shifts that always move me:

> You seem a tiny wrecked thing to me
> something sacred   where time has gone
> old and green

The elder poets of this anthology came of age immediately after World War II. Their generation had been primed by the great decades of European, North American, and Latin American avant-garde experimentation, which lasted from about 1910–39. Dada and Surrealism had brought a politics of the non-rational into poetry, seeing the modern nation-state as dependent on banishing patterns of thought and speech that didn't conform to a narrow sense of the human as an economic animal. Surrealists used a host of techniques to provoke a revolution that would open human consciousness to alternate realities: dream imagery, automatic writing, and collaborative writing practices that could create a single text out of many minds. They went for drug-induced visions, sought out African and Pacific tribal art, and cultivated a range of practices in order to break the grip of rational thought processes.

Russian Futurism and Constructivism—two other avant-garde schools—brought modern topics for poetry into the mix, along with new-found industrial insights into how things (including poems) get made. The Negritude poets—African and Caribbean writers composing poetry in French, the language of their colonists—subverted European conventions of speech. Performers among the Dada crowd and other groups influenced by contact with folklore and tribal traditions made poems out of sheer sound (the Futurists called them *zaum* poems). You could say that these explorations prepared the North American ground.

What came newly into the mix during the conservative and conformist years of the Eisenhower administration was an immediate and deeply informed contact with Asian poetry. A great deal of provocative material was being brought to North America by combatants, travelers, merchants, and journalists in the wake of the Pacific war—all of it giving a new reading to poetry experiments. Asian teachers and texts showed that deliberate traditions of spiritual wisdom had been using and safe-guarding for thousands of years a range of practices that used speech, image, and written language for spiritual purposes. One notable example can stand for the wealth of material: the mantra that closes the *Heart Sutra,* that most famous piece of Buddhist scripture. Its words are simple, clear, vague, impenetrable, or inherently meaningless depending on your perspective. It is introduced in the sutra as "the great bright mantra that relieves all suffering," and the fact that it remains in its original Sanskrit no matter what language the *Heart Sutra* has been translated into makes clear its magical and spiritual intent.

"The great mantra is given thus: *Gate gate paragate parasamgate bodhi svaha.*" (The Dalai Lama translates the first part of this "Go, go, go beyond, go totally beyond" and tells us the last two words can be conceived as (though not translated as) "be rooted in the ground of enlightenment").

Moving this direction in dramatic fashion was Michael McClure's discovery (rediscovery?) of what he termed "beast language." His 1969 underground classic *Ghost Tantras* is the primordial text. The book's title goes undefined but its back cover shows where the poems come from: "A dahlia or a fern might become pure speech in meditation. A woman's body might become the sound of worship. A goddess lies coiled at the base of man's body, and pure tantric sound might awaken her." 2500 years earlier the poet Bharata, a personal disciple of Shakyamuni Buddha, had left a poem that called to his comrades, "Come . . . / let's give the lion's roar / face to face with all buddhas." McClure's first ghost tantra could be a response—

GOOOOOOR! GOOOOOOOOOO!
GOOOOOOOOOR!
GRAHHH! GRAHH! GRAHH!
Grah goooooor! Ghahh! Graaarr! Greeeeer! Grayowhr!
Greeeeee
GRAHHRR! RAHHR! GRAGHHRR! RAHR!
RAHR! RAHHR! GRAHHHR! GAHHR! HRAHR!
BE NOT SUGAR BUT BE LOVE
looking for sugar!
GAHHHHHHHH!
ROWRR!
GROOOOOOOOOOH!

How close this gets to the esoteric tantras recited by American practitioners of Tibetan Buddhism! As with original Sanskrit and Tibetan texts, it moves between meaningless and meaning-laden words. Similarly, even the simple meal-time chants in the Zen meditation hall (brought from Japan) aren't too distant. They contain at least a few "meaningless" syllables hummed, purred, growled, or spat. Consider this passage I lifted at random from the *Candamaharoshana Tantra*, a text that goes back to at least the thirteenth century in India and was central to some of the more esoteric Buddhist schools. (I've arranged lines from the translation by Christopher S. George to resemble McClure's layout on the page.)

OM, Reverend Candamaharoshana, come come,
with all your family.
JAH! HUM! VAM! HOH!
Empower this mandala!
HUM! PHAT! SVAHA!
OM, Black Immovable, accept this flower!
HUM! PHAT!

I should note that the English words of McClure's ghost tantra are actually something of a "translation" from the *Gospel of Shri Ramakrishna,* a book originally written in Bengali and full of Bengal's mystical Hindu-Buddhist heritage.

The major texts of Buddhism throughout its history are the documents called *sutras*. In early Indian Buddhist traditions a sutra contained the remembered (and later recorded in writing) talks, dialogues, or sayings of the historical Buddha. In Mahayana Buddhism, the cosmopolitan flowering of Buddhism that began about 2000 years ago in India and the form of Buddhism that reached China, Tibet, and Japan, a sutra is spoken by any buddha (enlightened being). Thus the wealthy Indian layman and merchant Vimalakirti has a sutra. In China, Hui-neng, the Sixth Patriarch of Ch'an (Zen) Buddhism, has a strikingly popular one, with curious bits of possibly very old poetry bricolaged in. In eleventh century Japan, Eihei Dogen wrote several sutras, including "The Mountains and Rivers Sutra," read by many Zen adherents in North America today.

From the sutra literature of Asia came an impulse towards a certain kind of opulent or extravagant imagery in American poetry. In a few minutes I'll speak of the other tendency in American verse, which carries a drier tone, tends to regard anything sensational with suspicion, and distances itself from the overly speculative or the supernatural. But one direction poets have gone—and sutras provide the permission—is to fill their books with flowers, gemstones, fur, leather, fragrances, clouds, and mountains shimmering with fruit-bearing trees, galaxies of crystal rainbows. And to conjure vast interrelated and inter-folded universes of nearly inconceivable dimension (that is, wide open spaces for the Mind). These sorts of mind-spaces appear throughout the present volume, notably in the unfolding of flowers, galaxies, and incessantly gestating mammals in McClure's poetry. In a drier, more folkloric way they appear in Eliot Weinberger's prose poems drawn from Chinese history and legend.

One of the first sutras composed on the North American continent (and called a sutra) was Gary Snyder's 1969 "Smokey the Bear Sutra." Drawing from Indian models it included notable use of the Sanskrit mantra:

Namah samanta vajranam chanda maharoshana
Sphataya hum traka ham mam

"I DEDICATE MYSELF TO THE UNIVERSAL DIAMOND—
BE THIS RAGING FURY DESTROYED"

Written for the attendees at a Sierra Club Wilderness conference in Oakland, California, it collapsed centuries and continents by identifying Smokey the Bear with Fudo Myo'o, a wrathful Buddhist deity who may have himself once gotten overlayed upon a prehistoric bear deity of Japan. Snyder's interest in deep time, and its relation to Buddhist doctrine, permeates all his poetry. So does the playfulness that in this case brings Forest Service icon Smokey the Bear into the mix.

Allen Ginsberg wrote a sutra too, the "Wichita Vortex Sutra." His is more gloomy in tone than Snyder's. The poem takes its sounding at the geographical center of the United States (Wichita, Kansas) and in Whitmanic fashion studies and details the spiritual condition of the United States during the Vietnam War from the window of a Greyhound bus. Another American sutra, modeled closely on Mahayana Indian originals, is Jack Kerouac's *Scripture of the Golden Eternity.* Kerouac composed the little volume at the behest of friends who thought his long-time Buddhist studies should be put directly into sutra form. Another of Kerouac's works picks up on the mystical language of India, and the vast inter-galactic dimensions: *Old Angel Midnight.* It is an explicitly Buddhist meditation in language. Throughout its pages it emits seed syllables that bring nonsense and prayer together—

Pirilee pirilee, tzwé tzwa tzwa,—tack tick—
birds and firewood. The dream is already ended and we're
already awake in the golden eternity.

This kind of language was right in the tradition. Sutra literature often holds, as though cobbled in by early collage artists, a variety of gatha, mantra, and dharani. Scholars regard these curious, antique artifacts as fragments of quite old verse (some of it certainly predates Buddhism) that have found their way into Buddhist texts compiled centuries later. Contemporary artists would say these bits of old poetry are "cut in"—the terms collage or *bricolage* are used by poets, or the more colloquial phrase "cut-up."

All poets, and of course all those in this book, use *sound-magic* strategies, whether explicitly and boldly, or subtly and with a hidden hand. Leslie Scalapino's "it's go in quiet illumined grass land," because it's one of the more opaque poems here, deserves a moment's attention. The title—a phrase that recurs in variants throughout the poem—gathers its mystery and effect from repetition and half-echo. The poem does not so much set non-sensical or meaningless language spinning as some of the poems mentioned previously, but it will defy the reader unless you give deep regard to its use of recurrent phrases. (We must not mistake *recurrence* for *repetition*: when a phrase recurs it produces a very different effect the second time around.)

Always stay in
the quiet illumined grass
land — but I can't — do it
there being other people there
to
just do
it only staying in the grass land
illumined
'place' it together is 'land' and
comes out
just
do it

Could this phrase (this place for the mind to dwell)—"quiet illumined grass land"—mark the emergence in our North American literature of a previously unknown paradise or buddha land, as though Amitabha Buddha's Western paradise has been restored and modernized for a secular society, with parks and open spaces providing respite from traffic and congested commercial districts? If so, circulation of the phrase "it's go in quiet illumined grass land" is a familiar technique. Consider the Tibetan prayer wheel, its circular phrasing that likewise repeats: *Om Mani Padme Hum.*

Contemporary typography might set the early Sanskrit and Tibetan mantra thus:

Let me give a personal reading to Scalapino's haunting but difficult poem. I'd been reading the pocket-sized book off and on for two years, but finally learned the authentic power of *it's go in quiet illumined grass land* on a wintry climb of South Arapahoe Peak (Southern Rockies, Indian Peaks Wilderness) last October. It was a day that icy winds came gusting over the Continental Divide, along which South Arapahoe's summit lies. Much of the mountain was covered by snowfields, packed to unpredictable depths by constant wind, slick on the surface, fatiguing, and in places treacherous to walk across. The viable footing was along interconnected patches of high steep meadow grass, swept free of snow by the wind, and lit across its mat-like surface by sunlight. The ice-covered talus that had tumbled down from the ridge, and the troublesome snowfields with their blinding solar reflection, could be avoided only by winding along the exposed grasslands. The phrase "it's go in quiet illumined grass land" quite literally kept my oxygen-deprived mind in focus, my feet on the grass, and led the way up the mountain on a day the wind-driven snow was turning so much of the slope perilous. I recommend it for mountain pilgrims!

Harryette Mullen's "Mantra for a Classless Society" also makes use of language with non-conventional syntax, though it works on the reader differently. Here it is the eruption of oral, ironic, African-American critiques of power into the patterns of the dictionary. Syntax and grammar are gone; what occurs is a troubling but necessary focus for the mind. A mantra after all is quite literally in its Sanskrit etymology a "mind-focusing device."

> penniless penurious poor
> poverty-stricken embarrassing
> upsetting awkward ill-at-ease
> nervous self-conscious tense

Similarly Mullen's "Xenophobic Nightmare in a Foreign Language," with its painful iteration of the phrase "bitter labor" (indefinable, but we all feel in our muscles what it means), has a similar effect. It highlights through use of acidic irony (and a nineteenth-century American legal document) the Second Noble Truth. Suffering has a cause—in this case social and political, judicial and bureaucratic—not so much to be defined (thus explained, made abstract, turned into a vacant non-magical phrase, and manipulated by lobbyists). It is instead to be brought into the reader's personal field of experience.

How many times can you read the recurrent phrase "bitter labor" tangled in cold legalese before it exposes the cruelties of government policy? In Mullen's poem the phrase feels like the *PHAT!* of Tibetan tantric texts, a very physical expulsion intended to dislodge tightly held delusions from the practitioner's mind.

Spell and mantra, prayer and dharani, chant and curse. When a community of people use these regularly—within the context of their daily activities—are we not talking about oral poetic performance as a component of life? Anthropologists and scholars of ancient literatures suggest the origins of drama lie in community ritual. I would guess the origins of much ceremonial language are similar, and the regular use of oral formulae means people are living their lives inseparable from poetry. Surely with this thought we come into range of the Zen Buddhist notion that the shape of one's life is a work of art.

Not far from these thoughts (edging a little closer to the mind-cracking paradoxes or illogical formulations of Zen koan literature) are the provocative directions for art given in Shin Yu Pai's "Yes, Yoko Ono."

Yoko Ono's Zen-inspired avant-garde writing in her 1970 *Grapefruit* are for some of us an underground classic. The book has been continually in print but I've never heard a scholar speak of it. No doubt it is too foxy a text; I have watched children read it with deep concentration, but it eludes the subtle thoughts of literary professionals. Shin Yu Pai's pieces—a tribute to Yoko Ono—are directives for possible art projects the reader can perform. But these performance-art instructions are intended to lead us far past the borders of logic, reason, good citizenship, or even material possibility. They are calls to action (ceremony or ritual?) that include the sky, a herd of sheep, and other citizens of the non–human world, as participants. Not speech reduced to its magical elements as in mantra—these "pieces" (as Shin Yu Pai calls them) go the other way. The natural world, unable to meet the freedoms of speech, mind, and imagination, gets reduced to words. Once that occurs, the world becomes as malleable as thought (recall William Carlos Williams: "A new world is only a new mind"). And the life of the spirit appears more free, and way more playful, than before—

Sheep Piece

Borrow a herd of sheep,
one hundred in number or more
spray paint their fleece
with your favorite words.
Watch from a distance as the sheep
arrange themselves into poems.

I find "Sheep Piece," and all of Pai's work, curiously close to T'ang Dynasty Chinese poet Han Shan, who I give here in translation by Red Pine (Bill Porter)—

raise a single cow
she will bear five calves
the calves will bear calves too
your herd will never end

tell Lord Chu of T'ao
you're just as rich as him

. . . .

Thus far I have made a few brief excursions into what we might get from wild animal howls, occult or spiritual spells, nonsense calls, and the types of language-magic that occur in this anthology's poems. Most of these ways of physically engaging poetry, through the possible but frequently unused applications of the human voice, were prefigured in the early twentieth century by the avant-garde writers of Europe and the Americas. With the gradual appearance in North America of a Buddhist science of language—advanced to sophisticated limits by tantric practitioners of India and Tibet—additional explorations within poetry have opened up. You could say that through poetry one might scour the six realms of existence. The human voice leads the mind, and the paths it takes enter realms inhabited by animals, ancestors, ghosts, spirits, deities—and buddhas. Yet poetry can take other directions.

Tending in a paradoxically different direction is the influence that comes to North America from classical Chinese poetry. The Western discovery of Chinese poetry has probably exerted the greatest effect of the past ninety years on North American verse, and provided the gate to Buddhist study for several generations of poets and readers.

Two thousand years ago, when Buddhist practice entered China (already a great and ancient civilization) and encountered Daoist and Confucian ideas, it generated an unprecedented flowering of culture. Some think this set off the greatest unfolding of poetry in world history. Intertwined with the rise of Ch'an (Zen), a specifically Chinese form of Buddhism, the masterful poetry of China's T'ang Dynasty (sixth to ninth centuries) and Sung Dynasty (ninth to eleventh centuries) came into existence. Ch'an masters and secular poets developed their work together, exchanging ideas, philosophies, and yogic techniques. They drank tea together, practiced calligraphy and painting as adjunct arts, and swapped thousands and thousands of poems. (One official anthology holds 50,000 poems, and hundreds of poets each left hundreds of pages behind.) Several of China's finest poets—Su Tung-p'o and Wang Wei among the better known—were recognized adepts of Ch'an Buddhism.

The formative translations into English—the ones that brought an unprecedented shift in Western approaches to poetry—were the fifteen poems, later increased to seventeen, published by Ezra Pound in 1915 under the title *Cathay.* Most of Pound's poems derived from T'ang Dynasty poet Li Po; all came via the notebooks of Boston art scholar, collector, and curator Ernest Fenollosa. Fenollosa, who Pound never met, had studied Chinese poetry with several Japanese scholars in Japan, and had left at his death a series of careful notebooks. From these Pound, with little other information about Chinese poetry and no one to guide him, put together his translations. T.S. Eliot at the time made a famous pronouncement, that Ezra Pound had "invented Chinese poetry" for our time. The statement sounds a bit patronizing, even neo-colonial, to contemporary ears.

What Pound actually did was to change American poetry forever, by introducing tones of voice and ways of writing that seemed waiting to arrive. More modestly, he ushered in a century-long practice of American poets translating the master poets of Buddhist and Daoist China, and of course getting their translations into the hands of readers. Pound's work from the Chinese introduced a clarity or directness of expression suited to the twentieth century. After long years of Western poetry modeled on figures of speech, on rich tapestries and epic adventures, on symbolism, and wrapped in patterns of rhyme and metrics that had nothing to do with how people actually speak, a new tone arrived.

To demonstrate the change, here's the first stanza of "Ballade of the Chinese Lover," published in 1899 by American poet Stuart Merrill. That its theme is Chinese (and its supposed speaker Chinese) ought to make clear how irrelevant both Chinese and American poetry would have seemed in either New York City or the coal-mining camps of Colorado.

Down the waves of the Yang-tse-Kiang,
  In a gilded barge with saffron sails,
I wooed my Li to the brazen clang
  Of kettledrums, and the weary wails
  Of flutes, whilst under her spangled veils
She would sway her willowy waist, and sing
  Sweet songs that make me dream of dales
Of Han-Yang, Woo-hoo and far Tchin-Ting.

Ezra Pound, sixteen years later, as his European friends left for the trenches of France during World War I—

Taking Leave of a Friend

Blue mountains to the north of the walls,
White river winding about them;
Here we must make separation
And go through a thousand miles of dead grass.
Mind like a floating wide cloud,
Sunset like the parting of old acquaintances
Who bow over their clasped hands at a distance.
Our horses neigh to each other
as we are departing.

Other fine translations in the wake of Pound's came from the British poet Arthur Waley, the American Witter Bynner, and with terrific influence on Americans after the Second World War, from Kenneth Rexroth. All of them combined to introduce an intimacy of tone—once compared in China to "gnawing on withered wood"—that is deliberately non-sensational, somewhat dry, unsentimental in its approach, and results in a poetry that sounds as though one reasonable person were conversing intimately to another.

This tone originated with T'ao Ch'ien (365–427) who poet-scholar Eliot Weinberger says was "the first to describe ordinary experience in plain speech" in his poetry. This created the intimate lyric voice that distinguishes classical Chinese and makes it sound so contemporary. T'ao Ch'ien's poems have an unassuming surface, but under the surface reveal rich strata of thought. Here is the quote by Huang T'ing-chien, five hundred years after T'ao: "When you've just come of age, reading these poems seems like gnawing on withered wood. But reading them after long experience in the world, it seems the decisions of your life were all made in ignorance."

However dry the poems sound, their emotions run deep. Classical Chinese poems are about friendship, the parting of friends, the perils of life under conditions of war, unjust social conditions, hard work, affection for family, the uncertainties of travel. Mountains and rivers—the wide natural world—became the observable setting, with poets regularly setting off into distant peaks in search of elusive Buddhist hermits. Most of the poems address themes that were immediate to China's every day life, themes we understand without a moment's hesitation a thousand years later.

Some of the wilder-minded Chinese poems carry koan-like elements. Some include Daoist alchemical lore, or occult Buddhist imagery. A bit of all this can be found in the poems of Han Shan—"Cold Mountain"—a T'ang Dynasty poet who most likely lived in the seventh century. This half-legendary wild man of Zen deserves a shrine of his own in the Sierra Nevada. In 1956 Gary Snyder published in *Evergreen Review* a set of twenty-four Han Shan poems with a brief introduction. These have become some of the more influential poems of our era. They come to you like this:

In a tangle of cliffs I chose a place—
Bird-paths, but no trails for men.
What's beyond the yard?
White clouds clinging to vague rock.
Now I've lived here—how many years—
Again and again, spring and winter pass.
Go tell families with silverware and cars
"What's the use of all that noise and money?"

Snyder's collection, reprinted numerous times in the volume *Riprap and Cold Mountain Poems*, became a kind of handbook-in-the-rough for a generation called to a blend of Buddhist practice, ecological consciousness, outdoor adventure, spiritual renunciation, and life on the margins of conformist North American society.

Jack Kerouac's 1957 novel *The Dharma Bums* (its central character modeled on Snyder) made that kind of life the hippest revolution around. Han Shan and his North American descendents sit at the spiritual center of Kerouac's book; the search for a perfect haiku is the poetic goal; the rugged snowcap mountains of Western North America have become the buddha land of accomplishment and enlightenment. And here, in these buddha mountains, the dry, slightly melancholy poetry of the Chinese masters meets American frontier know-how. Two cultures lock eyebrows, as the Zen books would say.

From T'ao Ch'ien's time on, the ideal in Chinese poetry was elegant simplicity. The phrase "gnawing on withered wood" sets the tone. This comes forward 1600 years to emerge in quite a few poets of this present anthology. I'd like to point out that a surprising number of them have not only learned from the Chinese masters, but have contributed fine translations of classical Chinese poetry: Gary Snyder, Sam Hamill, Mike O'Connor, Arthur Sze, Eliot Weinberger, and Shin Yu Pai. What does it mean that so many American poets have gone deep into China's poetry, learning the ideograms, studying the structure of the originals, and dedicating years of unpaid work to translation of the masters? At this point could one imagine our own poetry without the influence of Tu Fu, Li Po, Su Tung-p'o, Li Ch'ing-chao, and Wang Wei? If I open a current poetry magazine I hear Li Po but rarely John Dryden.

We hear the influence—or should I say we risk gnawing on withered wood—when we bite into poems by Snyder, Hamill, O'Connor, Pat Reed, Norman Fischer, and others. I think this is one of the prevalent stances of American poetry in our era. Jane Hirshfield's "Reading Chinese Poetry Before Dawn" makes explicit tribute not just to the poets she's gone to school with, but to the tone their poems set: ordinary experience recounted in plain speech.

Sleepless again,
I get up.
A cold rain
beats at the windows.
I ponder Tu Fu's
overturned wine glass . . .

. . . .

Literatures from the Tibetan plateau have been less formative for Americans. And I have heard nearly nothing about Mongolia, which developed a similar form of Buddhism to Tibet. Yet after the eleventh-century poet Milarepa became widely known in the West from W.Y. Evans-Wentz's 1951 *Tibet's Great Yogi Milarepa,* the premises of a wildly visionary, and profoundly instructional, Buddhist poetry became familiar. Milarepa's poems are distinctive for their precise articulation of subtle points of Buddhist doctrine.

With the settlement in North America of numerous Tibetan refugees (among them monks and lamas funded by Western disciples), there has been steady awareness of the *doha* (instructional) verse of Tibet. There has also risen a practical interest in philosophical discourse, inward states of mind reflected in poetry, and the speculative travels of human consciousness after death.

Milarepa and his fellow Tibetan singers had poetic roots in pan-Asiatic shamanism, in Himalayan folk traditions, as well as in Tantric Buddhist linguistics brought up from India from about the eighth century onwards. Gary Snyder spoke of Tibet's lore in his 1969 volume *Earth House Hold,* and passages from Kerouac's novels suggest something in Tibetan traditions excited him. In her biographical notes for this anthology, Shin Yu Pai credits an undergraduate college course for introducing her to Milarepa, and regards these poems as formative for her thoughts about Buddhism. Through much of Diane di Prima's poetry you can find elements taken from her personal studies with lamas, and her reading of such texts as the *Bardo Thodol* or *Tibetan Book of the Dead.* Her "Death Sunyata Chant" lands exactly in this tradition—

> If you will be judged by a bureaucratic god
> or wear golden shoes in the golden fields of the Lord
> or carry to death yr guilt about kinky sex
> If the faces you hallucinate *are* a last judgment
> *Everything is illusion*

Will Alexander's fifty-page poem "Asia," which I've been able only to exerpt in this anthology, draws upon the magico-spiritual elements of Tibetan poetry lore. It presents the Tibetan diaspora after the Chinese invasion, seen through the eyes of an African-American from East Los Angeles who is schooled in Surrealist and Negritude poetries. Alexander's poem's dense language, as well as its spiritual ferocity, come close to Euro-African Surrealism on the one hand, and on the other, the Tibetan song of yogins who inhabit a ruggedly austere, magical landscape. His poem could be laid alongside a song of Milarepa's to highlight the excited and exalted language common to both:

for us
the true interior Tibet
of dark and irreversible surcease
tearing down the dialectical habitat
with structures
from our darkened Bon endowment
kaleidoscopic with vermin
with spells
with fabulous eradications and wildness

The fullest use in this collection of Tibetan lore, Buddhist and otherwise, appears in Tsering Wangmo Dhompa's poems. Tsering was raised by her mother, an officer of the Tibetan government-in-exile at Dharamsala. She eventually moved to Nepal, the nation with the highest population of Tibetan refugees, attended college in India, and finally moved to San Francisco. One of the compelling qualities her poetry brings to the current scene is its background in the day-to-day life of Tibetan culture. Along with Buddhist liturgy and deeply held ceremony, this background includes the culture's folk and oral "literatures": many types of song such as nursery rhyme and childhood rhyme, courtship customs, prayer, mother-wit aphorisms, geographical and gardening lore, and jokes. In the following lines from her "Body as What is Remembered" the language is distinctly American, but the repertoire of material arrives via hundreds of years of Himalayan folk wisdom, literature, and cultural memory.

The place of death is unidentifiable. But the jackal's night song
is noticed.

I am not from the tooth-falling region of Nangchen. But my
father is.

Marigolds can be grown in an empty kerosene barrel. Egg shells
and soggy tea leaves applied as fodder.

. . . .

The other major expression of Buddhist-inflected literatures that threads through the poets in this anthology is that of Japan. Of contributors to this volume, both Sam Hamill and Jane Hirshfield have published important translations of Japanese poetry, as has Gary Snyder. Snyder, Joanne Kyger, Philip Whalen, Norman Fischer, Hamill, Scalapino, and others have traveled extensively or lived for significant periods in Japan, studying at monasteries, undertaking pilgrimages, and immersing themselves in the nation's poems, poetic diaries, travel journals, novels, and Noh and Kabuki plays. These writers and their comrades have been instrumental in naturalizing to this North American continent accessory practices: tea ceremony, flower arrangement, calligraphy, the circumambulation of mountains, and the building of shrines. One Japanese form of poetry, haiku, is for all these poets as old as ice, as common as breakfast.

Haiku, the brief Japanese poem of traditionally seventeen syllables, has two characteristics to note. One is its near universal identification with Zen practice and the cultivation of present-moment awareness. The other is that it is surely the best-known and most practiced form of poetry on the planet today.

In 1483, the Japanese monk and litterateur Ten'in Ryutaku wrote, "Outside of poetry there is no Zen, outside of Zen there is no poetry." But it was the powerful example of haiku and renga-master Matsuo Basho, two hundred years later, through which Poetry—particularly haiku composition—became a "Way." Through the force of Basho's influence, poetry became an explicit training-ground for *satori* (deep realization) like other disciplines already identified with Zen Buddhist discipline: calligraphy, painting, the tea ceremony, martial arts, flower arrangement—even pottery, basket making, dyeing, and other traditional, mostly rural crafts.

In China, Ch'an/Zen approaches to calligraphy had long maintained that the character of a man—his level of individual realization—could be observed in the *ch'i* or life-energy that moved through his brush and left an imprint of its passage in ink on the rice paper. The same Zen insight suggests to American poets that the practice of writing poems is not so much to make a thing (let alone to secure prizes, awards, or grants) as it is to trace the way the mind moves. In an often-quoted 1959 press release titled "Since You Ask Me," Philip Whalen wrote: "This poetry is a picture or a graph of the mind moving, which is a world body being here and now which is history...and you." He added, "I do not put down the academy but have assumed its function in my own person, and in the strictest sense of the word—*academy*: a walking grove of trees. But I cannot and will not solve any problems or answer any questions." The Philip Whalen poem that closes this anthology gives tribute to those early Chinese calligraphers, who lived for the energy they could direct across the page.

Similarly, poets have always regarded poetry as a Way, a path towards realization, though in Buddhist circles arguments have flown both for and against poetry. The Zen master (and uniquely candid poet) Ikkyu, writing in fourteenth century Japan, called poetry "a path to intimacy with demons." And back in China the superb Po Chü-i wrote during T'ang times (Burton Watson's translation):

> Since earnestly studying the Buddhist doctrine of emptiness,
> I've learned to still all the common states of mind.
> Only the devil of poetry I have yet to conquer—
> let me come on a bit of scenery and I start my idle droning.

I tend to think of these dismissive asides as tongue-in-cheek, as playful warnings for the unwary who may be more interested in recognition and Guggenheim awards, NEA grants, and Bollingen Prizes, than in a life-long wrestling with the dragons of syntax and sound. But with Basho's example a new approach, poetry-as-pilgrimage, appeared as an explicit alternative to careerism. (Even in Basho's Japan careerism in poetry had degraded the art.) The Way of Poetry became seen as a *practice* in and of itself. Moreover poetry draws a certain kind of practitioner—as Basho saw it—who is not exactly a priest, not exactly a layperson, but something other. The poet in his or her devotion to language and experience tries to realize the Unconditioned. From the Daoist perspective, such a practitioner approaches the realm of the "perfectly useless." "Poetry," wrote Basho, "is a fireplace in summer, a fan in winter. It runs against popular taste and serves no use." At the 1987 Green Gulch Zen Center conference on poetry and meditation, Philip Whalen (himself a Zen adept) said, "As far as meditation goes I'm a professional. I've been a professional since 1973. And that's my job. I find it very difficult to sell."

Basho had undergone some Zen training (how much, nobody knows) but was never ordained a monk or priest. He wandered in robes as a layperson—like a bat, he once described himself—neither bird nor mammal. He confessed in one of his travel diaries that he had "considered entering the precincts of the Buddha and the teaching room of the ancestors. Instead I've worn out my body in journeys as aimless as those of the wind and clouds, expending my feelings on birds and flowers."

The most famous of Basho's journeys, written up in his poetic travel journal *Oku no Hosomichi,* ("Back Roads to the Far Province of Oku" would be a clunky but literal version of the title for Americans) has become, through many good translations, standard reading for American poets. It is probably the case that, with the exceptions of Shakespeare and William Blake, no poet's work has been so widely considered by contemporary poets as this one slim book. Gary Snyder's *The Back Country* opens with an epigraph that is Basho's opening line (the poet Cid Corman's translation): "...So—when was it—I, drawn like blown cloud, couldn't stop dreaming of roaming, roving the coast up and down...."

Sam Hamill has translated the *Oku no Hosomichi.* Norman Fischer and myself have published books that deliberately echo Basho's title. Lawson Inada's "A Hi-Five for I-5" brings the impulse up to date on our own continent. Interstate 5 is one of the West Coast's major north-south arteries, linking Tijuana to Vancouver, Britsh Columbia (in this anthology it also shows up in Gary Snyder's "Really the Real"). Inada's poem is in style a *renga,* or linked-verse sequence, celebrating not just the transcontinental highway and its travelers, but the spirit of early Buddhism's *the path exists but not the traveler on it.* Its opening link—

> Archaeologists have determined
> that the I-5 Corridor
> was originally a Power Path
> with sacred Prayer Places
> accessible on the side.

In Japan a renga was generally the collaboration of several poets; up to a hundred might contribute to a one hundred-verse sequence over the course of several days. In time it became standard practice for a single poet to link verses into a sequence, changing the tone, topic, and season as the poem evolved. Pat Reed's "Container of Stars" is a loose approximation of the old form; the setting is a poet's pilgrimage into the

Sierra Nevada high-country of California. Her poem, breath-takingly compressed in its language, bristles less with the "low" or pop-culture language that haiku cultivated than Inada's sequence. Both poets, however, draw on the prior Japanese tradition.

. . . .

What of the poems here that offer something new or unprecedented for Buddhist art? The ones through which you can't trace impulses or origins to earlier Asiatic models? These perhaps should fire our passion the most. Such poems introduce a decidedly indigenous flavor to American Buddhism. Here, lest it be misconstrued, I want to say why I included Dale Pendell's "Amṛta," which at first glance looks like it might be an essay. You could say it flies free of the tenets of expository prose, however, and lifts the mind into new territory. This piece presents a surface that resembles prose scholarship, but belongs in this collection because it uses the best strategies of contemporary poetry. Pendell sets in motion multiple voices that dart from section to section (and sometimes coyote-wise contradict each other). It juxtaposes images according to non-rational or intuitive impulses, and in a collage-like gesture introduces foreign words and phrases including Sanskrit formulae and Chinese characters—hence visual devices and mystical chants cut across the page.

Pendell's devices remind me of Cecilia Vicuña's poetry, and the way she performs it. Vicuña—a visual and performance artist as well as a poet—works at the convergence of two continents, North and South America. Born in Chile, she left at the time of Salvadore Allende's assasination. As an ongoing tribute to native Andean traditions she works with *quipu*, the Incan culture's cord-writing that once used knots tied along a length of yarn or string as an alphabetical "writing." Vicuña draws the voices of Buddhist and other Asian texts into her writing, installation pieces, and performances. I have seen her prepare an "installation" in the room where she is to read her poetry aloud, stringing the space with twine, thread, or rope. She does this in dual homage, first to quipu, the archaic tradition of her homeland, and second to Buddhist literatures. *Sutra*, after all, in Sanskrit means thread (related to the English word *suture*) and *tantra* in Sanskrit is an "extending device," a loom, and refers to a weaving.

Drawing as haiku did from popular culture are two other poems I want to acknowledge for their distinctly American diction: Lawrence Ferlinghetti's "A Buddha in the Woodpile," and Tyler Doherty's "Bodhidharma Never Came to Hatboro." Perhaps these are homegrown prayers, recited in hope that Buddhist teachings bring to our civilization a wisdom it thus far lacks. Similarly attractive for their use of pop culture language are Hoa Nguyen's poems, which can hold the irreverence and humor of a Japanese Zen painting—

Buddha's ears are droopy   touch his shoulders
as scarves fly out of windows and I shriek
at the lotus of enlightenment

. . . .

As this collection goes to press the one poet included who is not counted among the living is Philip Whalen. I'd intended to select only from among the living, but Philip became the exception for several reasons. Significantly, he serves as a secret tutelary guardian to this book, a sort of curmudgeonly *dharmapala* (Sanskrit term meaning "protector of the teachings") by virtue of his ongoing presence in the poems, and in the lives, of many of the anthology's contributors. Kyger, Fischer, McClure, Sagan, and di Prima bring poems addressed to him. I might easily have chosen poems by Snyder, Doherty, Scalapino, Schelling, and others that invoke, praise, speak to, upbraid, or argue with Philip. His poetry has largely appeared from very small presses (the natural habitat of most American poetry), and is less widely known than it ought to be. A direct personal link connects him to Kenneth Rexroth, probably the first major American poet to embrace Buddhist poetry and philosophy in his own writing. Rexroth's translations from Chinese and Japanese poets are profoundly influential, and I hope one day Phil Whalen's poems will hold the stature in our nation that Su Tung-p'o's hold in China.

"Had we but world enough, and time," many other living poets would have gone into this volume. The list is too long to draw up—testimony to the roots Buddhism has now sunk in North America.

Somewhere Kenneth Rexroth wrote that the counterculture (in his view this would be the Dharma revolutionaries or the true culture-workers, in opposition to the depredations of mass culture and Capitalist/ Communist/Fundamentalist/Despotic/Anti-Nature/Anti-Woman systems of control)—the counterculture are those people, he said, who live their lives by the dictates of lyric poetry. The poets in this book do try to live their lives by the terms of their poems, and I hope you, the reader, will meet them there, with bravery, generosity, and humor. These poems are the original texts of an authentic American Buddhist life.

From Rexroth's "City of the Moon"—

Buddha took some Autumn leaves
In his hand and asked
Ananda if these were all
The red leaves there were.
Ananda answered that it
Was Autumn and leaves
Were falling about them,
More than could ever
Be numbered. So Buddha said,
"I have given you
A handful of truths. Besides
These there are many
Thousands of other truths, more
Than can ever be numbered."

This book offers a handful of poets. Besides these, there are many thousands of other poets, more than can ever be numbered.

Andrew Schelling
Boulder, Colorado
Year of the Wood Bird
February 2005

WILL ALEXANDER

WILL ALEXANDER was born in 1948 in South Central Los Angeles, California, and has lived there his whole life. He received a Bachelor's degree from UCLA "to little effect." In his early twenties he discovered the poetry of Rimbaud, Artaud, André Breton and the Surrealists, and Aimé Césaire's *Notebook of a Return to my Native Land*, along with the paintings of the modern colorists. He began to hang around Shams' Incense, at 85th and Broadway, the sole poet at an art collective of jazz musicians and visual artists. He credits K. Lyle Curtis, an older Los Angeles poet, "who had an international litmus" to his own work, with extending the range of his poetry. And he credits Clayton Eshleman, poet and editor of the influential journal *Sulfur*, with helping him see his writing as "not committed to the parochial scene." "My poetic frequency combines the subconscious, conscious, and supraconscious minds. A trebled level working over and beyond itself, combining language inspired by African animism, shamanism, and surrealism and its infinite conduits, infused with the incessant vertical motion of Aurobindo's 'Divine.'" Will works with pastel and pencil, and over the years has performed with musicians, most recently the guitarist Alan Sermerdjian in New York. Books of his poetry include *Asia & Haiti* from which the following is taken, *Towards the Primeval Lightning Field* from Leslie Scalapino's O Books, and *Exo-Biology as Goddess* forthcoming from Manifest Press. Will is the marketing manager for the press at Beyond Baroque, a Los Angeles-area poetry venue.

from ASIA

. . . through reasonings such as the
present birth's becoming a past
birth when the future birth becomes
the present birth, one identifies
that past, present, and future
births are mutually dependent and
thus do not exist inherently.

—JEFFREY HOPKINS
Meditation on Emptiness

You who are not imprisoned in the
flesh, who know at what point in
its carnal trajectory, its sense-
less comings and goings, the soul
finds the absolute verb, the new
word, the inner land . . .

—ANTONIN ARTAUD
Letter To The Buddhist Schools

The voice in this poem is a collective voice of rebellious Buddhist monks who hover in invisibility, vertically exiled, in an impalable spheroid, virescently tinged, subtly flecked with scarlet, conducting astral warfare against the Chinese invasion and occupation of Tibet. Their originating zone, "the great Sera Monastery, a focal point of anti-Chinese feeling, four miles" outside "of Lhasa."
—W.A.

"Let us recall the illusion:
the thousands murdered
the texts exploded
the sun become
a mechanical sub rosa

we
the once green wings of a magical Tibet
accused by the Maoists
by the exterior flames of ideology & assault

the insults
the curses
the fierce & poisonous scaling ores
endured
buried by general anthrax & demon

yet we've emerged
with our murmurs
with our saffron bleeding above the 12 illusive zones of the zodiac
with our bleak & tested fatigue
able to concentrate our blindings
our spectral condensation
to roaming steam
to tragic pints of venom

our fate ensnared
by Chinese materia
by dyslexic simian diversion

by we
of seeming maximal debility

the spiders swarming in our mantras
throughout this canticle of purges

we
exiled
in this green electrical penumbra
looking down
on this heinous
monochromatic Pentecost
on Marxist grafting
by furnace & foreclosure
pulled from our shrouded mantric chambers
to do wonders for the scions
for the misanthropic whaling dolls
stunted in their core by brutality

these drab & scaly Marxists
plotted by erasure
by procedure by burden
by churlish transposition of the conflagrant spirit sun

this has been our lot in exile
inside this magic virescent penumbra
spinning our prayer wheels
above our leaking opium explodents
above our fulgurant supernal yeasts

we
spawned from the ethers
by coupled monkey & demon
by incandescent boiling rods

so be it
in this primeval penumbra
in this heightened verdigris scarlet
in this incisive analogical omniscience
it is we

who break the bells wide open
it is we
who signal the dead in their post-mortem frenzy
with a turbulent flame of Yaks
with dense in-vital stuffing lynxes
with mixture by forboding & conundrum

for us
this is path by treacherous lightning analogy
by magic & blowing grass at the snow line

for us
the true interior Tibet
of dark & irreversible surcease
tearing down the dialectical habitat
with structures
from our darkened Bon endowment
kaleidoscopic with vermin
with spells
with fabulous eradications & wildness

so we are ensconsed
concentrated
with the non-rectangular
with savagery

we aspire to Nirvana
to be left unsullied
like vertical plumes
from a yurt on fire with potassics

we do not live in flotational scarlet
to dwell on Mesozoic geology
or speak of arguments & counter-arguments
concerning instinctive erasure & existence

so when we speak of the 'west-east' direction of the 'Pamirs'
or the 'Taurus Mountains along the southern edge of Turkey'
or the ashen 'edge of the Iranian Plateau'
it is the ligature of our throats
of our prognostic blazes

we whose empiric is vapour
whose high cylindrical interior
burns throughout a rudimentary balance
throughout a transparent hemlock

we in this floating Boschian domain
squalid
hierarchical
frenzied

* * * * * *

if we speak as mystic cannibals
or darkened scorpion dwellers from on high
it is because
we know existence to be nameless
to burn in flameless quaternary battles
fueled by opacity
by the thought of great hunger & schism

floating
'along the sacred circular road'
'past straggling files' of human pylon & kindling
'passing gardens' & 'orchards' & 'shaggy stretches of woodland'
we can't condemn our powers
or react with nervous blistering
as to our strange & unresolved galvanic catoptrics
therefore a rendezvous
a handicapped expression in the mind

we no longer act
with brazen optical breads
or the 'the red-capped Sarus crane'
always painted in Japan with beguilement

as if we relished
unembarkable cancellation
in each solemn fact of our electrical personae
as if we were rain
or drifting 'Cobalt Warblers'
summoned to withdrawal by inscrutable contradiction
giving the void an optics
a magical translation of prairies
throughout a flaming set of principles
from a partial bank
from a mistrusted foci

therefore
bramble as logos
surname as pontificate

we
who plunge
through inherent existence
who surmount as beast
restrictive gallstone as landscape
or asps who burn with thriving spittle

it is we who send up smoke through the archives
it is we who live in wakeless daylight threadings
so as to throttle the tincture of thankless monsters
so as to reach with our brooding the very chronicles of error

* * * * * *

the 'bombardment' began in the dark early hours
three meridians after the mortars

our hands peeled
our throats blown into rivulets

then the running stench of blood
the tumultuous ruination
by language conveyed in suppurating goiter
convective dolomites hurled as flesh through their targets of materia
the concretism blazing
& the seen & the unseen wandering between themselves as confused
& embittered mirages

here was Marx
here was the State
the inches geared by specific labour & yield
by the 'value' of 'value'
by technic peasant production
for all Mao's peasants were low
despicable
grinding
as the voice of crushed centipedes screeching from a lantern

& this in no way signals our cause
to take up ferocious measuring rains
to savour as our substance anachronistic dialectics

by March 23rd we were bloodily crushed
& given as praxis a life of leper's drills
of future as banquet of sorrow
as threnody
as requiem
as shelter under culpable acids & pain

we of enriched preambles of calm & non-motion
above a blank & imperceptible goddess
we Tibet
we the 'Glorius' suns of 'Learning'
famous for our teachings of the black & 'occult' arts

we
of the '100,000 Sermons' conclude
'There has arisen' from the depths the prime illuminator's power
'The Maker of Light who gives eyes to the world'
'Gotama'
'out of the miry pit'
who 'stands on dry ground'
'The Prince of Physicians'
master of corruption
floating above the mansions of angels transparent with sparks
with unpossessed infinities
Gotama
he who opens life beyond the plentitude of complexity
beyond the deadly perserverance whose name defies the prescence
of knavish opium caesuras

we
with top most reverence & honour
with our bloodless wings
with our meditative anthropometry
ensouling our balance
for the 'Judgement of the Dead'

we who breathe through terrible powers of clarity
are able to transmigrate through form
once as a flock of blood pheasants
then as a scale of singing demon fish
we who've ingested spells
from intensive Muru enchanters
from the monsters of scaly occult ravines
shaping our forms through osmosis
so as to transmute the scope of disaster
we
with our 'Depth of Body'
with our 'Breadth of head'
with our green 'Pharyngeal teeth'

because of such elliptical writhing
we called 'The leading oracles in Lhasa'
'the Nächung' & 'the Karmashar'
the masters
inflamed with clairvoyance from psychic citron ore

& we
Myrmidons of the 'Demon King'
came not as deficits
or as figments of a spare & misleading contagion
but as elements entranced by utter liquid as existence
with preternatural blazings
under kindled smoke
from a fire which formed from doubled cinnabar suns

we
the vortical base
the flammable adherents
here
our diagrams of loneliness go higher
than an Asiatic contour
than a broken interrogation

we
in this magic vessel
await our return to a transparent Lhasa
with its outpouring glare
with its incendiary chalice

we
of the old certitude of mantras
of lucid spell by arising
of incinerate & cascading ritual

it is we who compose on 'slabs'
'of black painted wood'

dusted with chalk & horizons
therefore composed
with blank symbolical scrawlings
risen above
the baneful bullion keepers
fulminate
as a luminous neurology of brilliance

then the senses hover in the deepest interiors of hearing
into musically wafted niveous elevation
tumulose
alpestrine
declivitous
incorruptable
candescent
powerful as to balefire & to plague
as to dense arcana & its ruses

we came to Nächung
for the solemn principle of learning
so as to live for each of the next substanceless eternities
to spawn confusion as to age
as to the place & time of our private spawning grounds
as to puzzle
crux
rebus
logogriph

we who bowed in dimness
at the throne 'of the great sorcerer'
& 'upon it lay his robes' & 'accoutrements'
'the great sword on the left'
'the magic breastplate' with its fires
the 'great brass cap loaded with gold'
of he who was possessed by the 'ferocious white monster'
with its 'three heads'

with its 'six hands'
atop
an apparitional 'white lion'

* * * * * *

we
of the rimless galaxies
we
of higher electrical intention
not concerned with the sun
or the fatal brew of its deadly 'helium ash'
but with other intensive reading diameters
with other eradications & species springing forth
with new inspired rotation gases

we
who negate the gravid
who summon forces
rapid & oracular with menace

we see the stars
through new calamity & adventure
we who see
with the sudden burst of an emptied luminosity

we exist
voracious with nullity & blankness
we who feast on flames from 'Saint Padma'
on rains from winged 'thunder bolts'

unlike the voice
from moaning burial vaults
we invoke the laloplegic as mantra
as magically soundless baryphony
thriving as we do
in this meteoritic spheroid

which hovers
which suspends itself in 'piercing' 'sapphire' skies
above the 'cinnamon sparrows'
above the 'red-legged crows' & the 'ravens'

unlike
the rough religious hymns
sung throughout 'Western Tibet'
we thrive on lightning
not like volatile monarchs
stuffing ourselves with asps for illusive provocation
nor like the hermits who plunge into wayward in-audia
with their 'rosary bits of human bone'
with their personal goblet cast from various skulls
we are neither of these races
stuttering as they do in chronicles of self-panic
as denial of excess
& excess against denial
none of these forces erode us
nor build from their cacophonies a syndrome
to harass us
or vanquish our seeming aloofness by spell

to the potentates we can say
that you've wasted your demons on envy
& to the ghostly tenants of caves we can say
that your sunless ferocity
is numbed by despotic branches on fire

we
of high magic
of timeless rectitude & cleansing
of fierce immunity & weaving
have burned up resistance
have scattered the laws
have torn down the prophets

we of new migration cycles
we of salt & blank ambrosial growings
of the life of vastitude
of interminate immensity & flying
are un-remitting
continuous
innumerable
undying"

TSERING WANGMO DHOMPA

TSERING WANGMO DHOMPA was born on a train halfway between Delhi and Chandigarh on March 6, 1969. She grew up in Dharamsala where her mother served as an elected member of the Tibetan Government-in-exile during its early days, then moved to Kathmandu when her mother resigned the post. She attended boarding school in Mussoorie (northern India) and completed Bachelor and Master's degrees in English Literature at Lady Shri Ram College, Delhi University. She worked as a feature writer for magazines in New Delhi for a year, then left Asia in 1995 to pursue a Master's Degree in Professional Writing from U. Mass and eventually a M.F.A. in Creative Writing at San Francisco State. For the past six years she has worked with the American Himalayan Foundation, located in San Francisco. The organization provides humanitarian aid to people in Nepal and Tibet, and to Tibetan refugees in India. She writes, "I believe in the basic principles and philosophies of Buddhism, and think of myself as a Buddhist...I think my writing returns to the questions or the day-to-day preoccupations with how to incorporate the philosophy within the practicalities of the modern day." Tsering is the author of *Recurring Gestures*, a chapbook from Tangram Press, and the book *Rules of the House* (Apogee Press) from which some of the following poems are drawn. Apogee will also publish *In the Absent Every Day* later in 2005. Tsering lives in San Francisco.

SUN STORM

Like brides behind veils, my people peep from drawn curtains and feel the air with their fingers. They do not see any use for heat and are not hospitable to it. Electric fans focus on bare shoulder blades and erect nipples.

Mosquitoes persist. Hands do not move fast enough.

On arrival, my people were instructed to throw away their black clothes, then taught to distract the sun. In crisp white pajamas and khadi shirts, they walked the camp till it paled to a canvas of gathering spirits.

Night led them to the edge of the stream. Feet in water, they talked about what they had left to lose.

Some afternoons, old stories were translated into Tibetan. *You are blessed*, strangers said. *God has delivered you. Such is his bountiful nature.*

Sparrows tattooed the air. Prayer beads clicked as mantras circulated above the parable of a son who erred and was forgiven. The story teller's lips bent with crystals of sweat.

Jesus loves you. For years, F thought Jesus was the president of a country. He thought he was a rich old man.

He told one story-telling woman she was wrong. Jesus had nothing to do with it. It was all fate.

HOW THUBTEN SANG HIS SONGS

You are adapted to speeches of silence, speak he said, speak.

Magpies shuffled in the neighbourhood as the world opened noisily. Empty tongues are so heavy, I said. What do you know of life, you who live in the cave?

Someone was getting married next door. A woman's giggle pierced the room. The world outside could not be kept out.

He summoned a milkman from the street. What causes you grief? Milk, said the man, milk.

He said to know where I was, I need to know where I came from. I could only hear one word at a time.

When I am with people, I am in love with people. When I am alone, I am alone.

What do you see in a cave when there is no light?

Shadows burn.

Fire.

Fire.

BARDO

A hundred and one butter lamps are offered to my uncle who is no more.

Distraction proves fatal in death. A curtain of butter imprints in air.

After the burning of bones, ashes are sent on pilgrimage. You are dead, go into life, we pray. My uncle was a man given to giggles in solemn moments.

Memory springs like crocuses in bloom. Self conscious and precise.

Without blurring the cornea, details are resuscitated. Dried yak meat between teeth. Semblance of what is.

Do not be distracted, Uncle who is no more.

He does not see his reflection in the river. The arching of speech over "s" as he is becoming.

Curvature of spine as it cracked on a misty morning. A shadow evades the wall.

You are no more, Uncle who is no more.

Every seven days he must relive his moment of expiration.
The living pray frequently amid burning juniper.

Communication efforts require the right initiative.

Somewhere along the line matters of motion and rest are resolved.

Crows pick the last offerings. You are someone else, uncle no more.

BODY AS WHAT IS REMEMBERED

The Year 2120. No reason why it should be remembered by a nation except that some lost their mothers. Nations mourn when they are reminded.

Existence is acknowledged when it is visible. Onion stains on breath. Deep coral rib. The place of birth ought to be important.

And would it have been different if the sea had been within normal vision? In the mountains, normal vision varies. Clear days begin on elemental blue. If one insists, there is more to see.

In a region of Nangchen, tooth life is short. Twenty year-olds are known to bare smooth gums.

What if the harbinger of birth was a rooster's shriek? If pink cheeks were not so unfashionable.

The place of death is unidentifiable. But the jackal's night song is noticed.

I am not from the tooth-falling region of Nangchen. But my father is.

Marigolds can be grown in an empty kerosene barrel. Eggs shells and soggy tea leaves applied as fodder.

Rain at an unlikely hour and hips were wet because there was so much bending.

Without a name the story could be anyone's. So there is a second name. And a third for the region you belong to if regions matter where you're from.

What comes out of your mouth is what you become. And if you don't speak, that too is worth noting.

AUTONOMY OF THE MIND

In my family, decisions are made by the lama
who dreams into fate. The husband who is rotten
whey is not as lucrative as the husband whose garden
grows tomatoes. After all, we're living through
a conjecture. Wiser to say sorry within the alternatives
of a moment and read the display of toes as assent.
Men are men because we know. The men in my family
hope to return to a country they left in their youth.
They say "home" and point away from the brick rooms
they have built. At home they say the grass was tall,
the milk was sweet. At home, there was no need for sugar.

Legions under the deceit of summer happily
doff colours unpurposeful as dandruff.
The neighbourhood you like will have flowers.
The bridge of your childhood will fall into the river.
Such things happen. We've made time into a chronology
usurping someone else's bed. What must we fight for?
The sum of a person's life is a precarious calculation
for the rat in the research room. We court our shackles.
We sharpen our tongues. Milk is on sale. The seven bowls
in our shrine are full of water. We're wearing skin
of ignorance and eyes that will not forget.

The youngest in the family died during the year of his obstacle.
A pilgrimage to four holy sites and seven offerings to lamas
proved otiose but Doma, the family dog, survived a fall from a steeple.
Once a year, our neighbhourhood girls worship their brothers
with offerings of flowers and vermillion powder, remembering
that brothers will one day take wives. We wish to know the ordeals
of all beings we pray for. Amphibians. Crocodiles. What of
oranges hanging like bats, their discomfort in being ripe?
What perpendicular roots we've formed, in this, our neighbour's
mother land. The departed will return but that is not necessarily good.
To be born a human is a commendable feat, the elders say,
marking our foreheads with black soot to keep evil eyes away.

To repine reasonably one must have a sense of humor.
The function of the earth is to be constant and to enfold.
This we understand when we learn to walk. In the mountains
there are stories of men who walk in air, the same men
also draw water out of rocks. You can call us creative;
we entreat our deities for rain and seek the almanac
before we listen to announcements made by the king
in transition. Let's keep the ceremony of little ones
this month; the ritual for the dog, the ritual for money.
Who will supplicate before the male deities in bronze
and in whose language? What will he say when it's all over?

If we are to learn well we must have faith like our mothers
who pray for the happiness of a world they have never seen.
A villain is the man in the film whose intention is to harm
and kill and is resurrected in the next show. A pillory exists
for him as the rehearsal of one more apology is staged
but the logic is often faulty. The death of family members is
not uncommon in my mother's family but most of them were killed.
Still, it's karma so there is no reproach. We pray for
what we are to eat in our mother tongue. We walk around relics.
In this life of our lifetimes, we learn not to use a headache
on an ordinary day to postpone judgement but we are not to judge.
Our mothers say life is simple because they've learned to ignore it.

Summer again; there should be no surprises after
having lived this long. Still, all confirmation of life
remains outside. A silver fish wanders under the desk.
We don't stop to wonder if it will live beyond the day.
Too much water in a person has lead to death. Water,
beyond these hills of concrete. My pockets are bereft
of practical jokes. They carry no use to sprouting
dandelions. Anemia has taken many of our strong women.
How are you? How are you? No sadness in practical tasks.
Paper as anchor. Replies made to people unknown.

After the night

She is afraid shadows will reveal indignities she has escaped
as light evades her room. That sorcerers will lift their skirts
and send thoughts to stick to her like damp leaves. She gathers
her belongings before sleep, thinking this will be the night to explain
matters of the past. It is rarely fear we leave behind in childhood.
A paper barely holding her name and address, just in case;
this she puts near her pillow night after night. The fear of the resolute;
like armies marching into a blind night singing love songs.
She wonders if protection comes from prayers.
In the morning she laughs, calls herself a silly thing and the night
is forgotten. Or accepted as an advantage. Far away in the future
of her tongue are promises of condiments. Turmeric. Saffron.
Of nights irresponsible as statues in the bazaar. These are
pledged. Surely we can live again and again through the same lesson.
In her dream comes a mother who has lost her street address.
She speaks no English and holds a key.

By the wayside

Mrs. Dhondup says life is not a happy lollipop
and she has said that before. Not in so many words
but when her brother lost his house in a neighbourhood fire,
and she went out to save what she could; while he went
to his buddies and drank himself to sleep—she said
she was, "washing her hands off his affairs." Then next morning
was seen cleaning the yard of embers. She is sitting with mother
who upon losing her composure is crying into her hands,
"Really, I would understand everything, if he would only..."
Somehow I always lose her last words. They are seated before
the window; how still the world is beyond mother's shaking
shoulders and Mrs. Dhondup running back and forth
between tea on the stove and cleaning rags which she puts
against mother's cheeks. She taps her finger against the window
to dislodge the ant walking on the outside. She points towards it
and it becomes the object of their compassion. Mother looks at the ant,
and beyond it to endless minutes, anticipating a lesson. Life is not
a happy lollipop,
she says. She looks towards me. Her fingers reach
for the window as though to wipe away the image before her.
It is her own but she is looking at something else.

Summer in Nangchen

Infant flowers bully
flies baking in the sun.
Summer's dust – masking all
forms. I am blinded temporarily;
when shapes appear, the greenest
of grass and men on horses.

After rain
Sounds implode,
flies that groan like giant bees.
And the ground, half wet—half dry
frenzy with legged beings.
Hair freed from its braid. Light
Footed as dust.

Liminal responses and how
sky and water emerge.
Not as evidence but duty to life.
Hot days lead me to the river's
edge. Rocks plump and plush.
Water warm and muddied stillness.
Then, a bird startles.

Wind through
turnip fields. Flies
a tizzy, float
in a witch's
dreaminess.

And the old lady
walking on her three legs
stumbles; gathers
and throws her ankles into motion.

Colour as necessity;
its occurrence must proclaim
or else remain step-sister.
I am writing in the dark through
shadows of my grandmother's
kitchen. Its pillars
an ancient ritual on my face.
Outside, clouds have taken over.
Gray drizzle; wet buttocks.
The mangy dog follows with a limp.

DIANE DI PRIMA

DIANE DI PRIMA, born in 1934 in Brooklyn, and educated at Swarthmore College, has published more than forty books of poetry, fiction, plays, and memoirs. In 1961, living on Manhattan's Lower East Side she began co-editing the magazine *The Floating Bear* with LeRoi Jones, and at this time was introduced to the classic literature of Zen. She was also instrumental in the foundation of Poets Theater in New York. She relocated to San Francisco in 1968 where she undertook study with Shunryu Suzuki Roshi, newly arrived from Japan. In 1974 she joined Allen Ginsberg and Anne Waldman in Boulder, Colorado, helping found The Jack Kerouac School of Disembodied Poetics at The Naropa Institute. She has remained a regular instructor at Naropa over the years, as well as co-founding and teaching in New College of San Francisco's Masters Program in Poetics. In 1983 she became a formal student of Chogyam Trungpa, Rinpoche. A scholar of alchemy, Western occult traditions, Asian texts, and Modernist poetry, she has also written some of the most influential political poetry of modern times: "the only war is the war against the imagination!" Some of her notable titles include the popular *Revolutionary Letters* published by Lawrence Ferlinghetti's City Lights Books, *Dinners and Nightmares*, and more recently a volume of memoirs *My Life as a Woman.* Recent poetry titles include *Pieces of a Song: Selected Poems* and *Loba, Books I and II*, a long poem begun in 1971. She lives in San Francisco where she teaches privately.

THREE "DHARMA POEMS"

1.
his vision or not?
gone is the authority
w/which he opened his fan.

2.
raindrops melt in the pond
& it's hard to say
just what "lineage" is

3.
my faith—
what is it
but the ancient dreams
of wild ones
in the mountains?

TO PHILIP WHALEN, 1999

I THREW IT OUT

all the typesetting I did of
"On Bears Head"   for
Poets Press
                    (it took me 2 yrs
                    to do it)

Threw it out. I was so mad.
you chose
                    Big Press &
                    $1500   over
                    us.

Wish now I'd kept it.
At least it had
                         all yr little
                         Squiggles &
                         drawings

painstakingly pasted in.
                         right into the poems
                         like you had em

Only today, 32 yrs later &
reaching for that book to show a student

I notice
the Big Press in NYC
left nearly all of them
                    OUT

wish now
I had that paste-up

gone

in a trash can
in Millbrook

I was so mad.

TASSAJARA, EARLY 1970'S

It was the sound mostly
the wooden han
huge antique drum from Japan
the stream singing over the stones
the dinner bell
swish of zoris
occasional wind rattling yucca on the hill
it was the sound & the silence
the way the daddy-long-legs moved on the white walls of the baths
a string quartet
of stringy silent legs

It was the fish-shaped bell,
the rustle of robes, the metal disk of the gong
the huge bell like a bowl, the songs of frogs
the occasional car grinding softly to a stop
  on the gravel of the parking lot
the thud of footsteps over the wooden bridge

It was the echo of voices already gone
they hung on the air:
Suzuki watering the rocks "so they wd grow"
Trungpa & his young wife talking in the garden
the thump of huge mallets making mochi
  in a hollowed-out tree stump
to the rhythm of Japanese & American folksongs
on New Years' Eve

It was the chanting that rose & fell like waves from the zendo
Crickets among the lanterns that outlined the paths
It was the small silver bell that clanged you awake

in the dark & the young monk running by as he rang it
& the slivers of sound small stars made sliding home

as you walked to the morning zendo thru tatters of night sky

I FAIL AS A DHARMA TEACHER

I don't imagine I'll manage to express Sunyata
in a way that all my students will know & love
or present the Four Noble Truths so they look delicious
& tempting as Easter candy. My skillful means
is more like a two by four banging on the head
of a reluctant diver
I then go in and save—
what pyrotechnics!

Alas this life I can't be kind and persuasive
slip the Twelve-part Chain off hundreds of shackled housewives
present the Eight-fold Path like the ultimate roadmap
at all the gas stations in Samsara

But, oh, my lamas, I want to
how I want to!
Just to see your old eyes shine in this Kaliyuga
stars going out around us like birthday candles
your Empty Clear Luminous and Unobstructed
Rainbow Bodies
swimming in and through us all like transparent fish.

IN THIS LANDSCAPE

In this landscape conspicuous for nothing but dust
& the lay of the sparse land
sharp smells shoot like lust across the crystalline forms
of black buildings.
                                        In this land where a 4 inch plant is all the hope
all the Buddha nature one wants
and drinking water costs $2/bottle

what chimes what bells what ghanta what intent
what touch what breath what mantra what good will
what words sung chanted shouted prayed or whispered can now
undo the disguise that has permanently disfigured
like soot our eyes   our hands   our hearts
what might
yet stir us   glimpse   glimmer

NEW YORK CITY, 1994

FOR SUZUKI ROSHI

after you died I dreamed you were at my apartment
we ate soba together, you giggled & slurped a lot

you said "Don't tell them I'm not dead"
& pointed down the street toward the Zen Center
"I don't want them to bother me."
We laughed & drank the broth.

I kept that promise: I think they still don't know.

DEATH SUNYATA CHANT:

A RITE FOR PASSING OVER

"Everything is illusion
but I am confident that all is well."

—"Hidden adept" from Tibet
quoted by Sogyal Rinpoche

If there is a Pure Land
we release the spirit
send it flying
into the Buddha's heart

Everything is illusion

If there are angels
will they carry you
singing
into the Presence?

I am confident

If the flesh is light & the fire
is a lover
If the ashes are scattered at sea
on the wind or planted in the earth
If all the five elements
are Wisdom Dakinis

and I am confident that all is well

what shape
    size
    glaze
will you take
in the potter's hands?
what realm
emerge in?

If the paths of the bardo are glorious
or frightening
if the light & sound is deafening
overwhelming
everything is illusion

If there is only extinction
& total dark
If we cycle thru forms throughout
the galaxy
If we must now return to Sirius
continue our Evolution
I am confident
that all is well

If you will be judged by a bureaucratic god
or wear golden shoes in the golden fields of the Lord
or carry to death yr guilt about kinky sex
If the faces you hallucinate *are* a last judgement
Everything is illusion:

the bodhisattvas
        adepts
the magick teachers
        lotus paradises
        pearly gates
& all the realms of Satan

the name of confusion & the name of wisdom
both blow away on the wind

the night of Brahma lasts a thousand aeons
the worlds are born & die
                sixty times a second
Valhalla & the sky of the Ghost Dancers
the spiral journeys under other stars
all shift & fade
flicker & re-emerge

they are all
an ancestral Dream Time

do you see?

the black air
that rattles in the back of yr throat
is transparent
a window on an unspeakable
dance

        vortex of Isis
                Shiva
                Hayagriva
                Olokun

the ambrosia of Kali is just this bitter taste
bile at the back of the tongue

awareness focuses as the vision fades

> *everything is illusion*
> *but I am confident*
> *that all is well—*

TRAVEL POEM

FOR SHEPPARD

leaving on a ten day trip
I get back in bed
for the warmth & to feel
your leg against mine

when the time comes
how will I ever leave this world
at once & without
looking back?

TYLER DOHERTY

TYLER DOHERTY was born in Toronto, Canada in 1973 and lives in the Germantown section of Philadelphia with his wife Michelle. Bird watcher, train rider, scribbler, and inveterate walker, he teaches composition at Arcadia University and co-founded with Leif Gustavson the Young Writers Project which conducts writing workshops with inner city Philadelphia youth. Inspired by R.H. Blyth's four-volume haiku translations, Chinese and Japanese poetry, Philip Whalen, and the example of Japhy Ryder in Jack Kerouac's *The Dharma Bums*, he started practicing Zen in the early 1990s before spending a a little over a year at Zen Mountain Monastery in residential training where he ate, slept, sat, walked, worked, and rang large bells. He holds a M.F.A. from Naropa University's Writing and Poetics Program—studying with Jack Collom, Reed Bye, Anne Waldman, Anselm Hollo, Michael Friedman, and Andrew Schelling—as well as degrees from McGill University (B.A.) and Arcadia University (M.Ed.). He currently practices with Barry Magid and the sangha of the Ordinary Mind Zendo in New York City. Poems have appeared in the *@ttached document 1 & 2* and *Shiny*. His first book of poems, *Bodhidharma Never Came to Hatboro,* was published in 2004 by Bootstrap Press.

BODHIDHARMA NEVER CAME TO HATBORO

The angel on your shoulder
has quietly disposed of the monkey on your back
with a little help from
the voice inside your head and the frog
in your throat
thought's all bark no bite
ever-seductive hurly burly
signifying nothing arf arf
just like the sound of a dump truck
but hard to see that way like
landscape consciousness in Chinese poetry
not useful to call either
'subjective' or 'objective' since
it's all mind
from word go
but oh never mind!
get your shoes on and let's get out of here
before I figure everything out
once and for all
temperature finally dropped after
past few days in the hundreds
including yesterday's red-white-and-blue
extravaganza bottle rockets pinwheels roman candles
as I contemplate death by golden oldie 98.1
no fate worse than Smokey Robinson
and the Miracles or high drama of a nearly hysterical Meatloaf
who would do anything except shut up
for love as we float in bathwater warm pool
trying desperately to be the ninth caller in
race windup orange fish and green frog
across the widest point from lay lows and

the mourning dove gives new meaning to the phrase 'wall-gazing'
as she sits on her new brood in a renovated sparrow nest
set between back porch cross beams
not moving not even blinking so long
her eyelids fall off
sitting in the nest
is its own time hatching is its own time
yellow flowers on the pepper plant
steering wheel's too hot to touch

5:VII:02 (4:04 PM)

RAVEN'S REVENGE

There was a time when I wouldn't
let squirrels or any other fuzzies
Rabbits Dogs Cats Woodchucks Skunks et al
into my Poems for fear they were too
cute—only birds allow'd
in this Tree House Private Keep Out
preferably serious ones with Sharp Talons
or Flesh-Tearing Beaks
definitely no Penguins Goonies or Ruddy Ducks but
Ravens were sufficiently mysterious I guess
because one poem ended that summer with a Wistfully Breathless
Tu Fu goes to Yoga Camp quaver—

"...and you carry mountains
rivers
in your beak..."

(it was about some Raven flopping off
into the distance—
Heroic Outlaw Variety Sunset no doubt—
after cutting it pretty close
to a rocky cliff)

& Anselm who knows ravens
almost before I'd even finished the
line had begun to rumble that

Subterranean Mutter-Chortle
his finely-tuned Preciousness Detector

registering off the charts as he sd

"Why don't you just
have the raven carrying Gary Snyder's
Mountains and Rivers book in its beak?!"

17:XI:02 (7:58 P.M.) FOR ANSELM HOLLO

LAWRENCE FERLINGHETTI

BORN IN 1919, Lawrence Ferlinghetti was placed in a New York orphanage after his father died and his mother went insane. From 1920–1924 he lived in France with a relative of his mother's, but eventually ended up in the custody of a family named Lawrence, from whom he probably took his first name. In the early 1950s he studied at the Sorbonne in Paris. When he returned to the States he settled in San Francisco, and in 1953 with a companion opened City Lights Books, the first all-paperback bookstore in the country. City Lights Publications, upstairs at the same historic location on Columbus Avenue in San Francisco's North Beach district, has published many of Ferlinghetti's peers, including *Howl and Other Poems* by Allen Ginsberg, which underwent a landmark trial for freedom of speech in literature. Ferlinghetti's own numerous titles of poetry include the best-selling *A Coney Island of the Mind*, many of its poems composed to be read to jazz accompaniment. Other titles include *Pictures of the Gone World*, *Endless Life: Selected Poems*, and *These are My Rivers*. Ferlinghetti has published novels, a celebrated account of a visit to Nicaragua during the Sandinista revolution, translations of the poetry of Jacques Prevert and Pier Paolo Pasolini, and is a prolific painter. A long-time civic activist in San Francisco, he spearheaded a drive to rename many of North Beach's streets after fellow poets, and served a term as poet laureate under Mayor Willie Brown. In the mid-1990s the city honored him by giving his name to a street that overlooks North Beach.

A BUDDHA IN THE WOODPILE

If there had been only
one Buddhist in the woodpile
In Waco Texas
to teach us how to sit still
one saffron Buddhist in the back rooms
just one Tibetan lama
just one Taoist
just one Zen
just one Thomas Merton Trappist
just one saint in the wilderness
of Waco USA
If there had been only one
calm little Gandhi
in a white sheet or suit
one not-so-silent partner
who at the last moment shouted *Wait*
If there had been just one
majority of one
in the lotus position
in the inner sanctum
who bowed his shaved head to the
Chief of All Police
and raised his hands in a mudra
and chanted the Great Paramita Sutra
the Diamond Sutra
the Lotus Sutra
If there had somehow been
just one Gandhian spinner
with Brian Willson at the gates of the White House
at the Gates of Eden
then it wouldn't have been
Vietnam once again

and its "One two three four
What're we waitin' for?"
If one single ray of the light
of the Dalai Lama
when he visited this land
had penetrated somehow
the Land of the Brave
where the lion never
lies down with the lamb—
But not a glimmer got through
The Security screened it out
screened out the Buddha
and his not-so-crazy wisdom
If only in the land of Sam Houston
if only in the land of the Alamo
if only in Wacoland USA
if only in Reno
if only on CNN CBS NBC
one had comprehended
one single syllable
of the Gautama Buddha
of the young Siddhartha
one single whisper of
Gandhi's spinning wheel
one lost syllable
of Martin Luther King
or of the Early Christians
or of Mother Teresa
or Thoreau or Whitman or Allen Ginsberg
or of the millions in America tuned to them
If the inner ears of the inner sanctums
had only been half open

to any vibrations except
those of the national security state
and had only been attuned
to the sound of one hand clapping
and not one hand punching
Then that sick cult and its children
might still be breathing
the free American air
of the first Amendment

NORMAN FISCHER

BORN IN WILKES-BARRE, Pennsylvania in 1946, Zoketsu Norman Fischer is a Zen Buddhist priest and prolific poet. He studied poetry at the University of Iowa, then attended the University of California, Berkeley, and the Graduate Theological Union. Ordained a Zen priest in 1980 he served as director of Green Gulch Farm Zen Center on the flanks of Mt. Tamalpais, and as Co-Abbot of the San Francisco Zen Center from 1995–2000, where he remains a Senior Dharma teacher. In 2000 he founded the Everyday Zen Foundation, with sanghas in Mexico and Canada as well as the United States. As a poet he has a distinct playfulness to his verse, indebted to a lengthy association with language poets of the San Francisco Bay Area. Most of his poetry has been published by small presses committed to avant-garde and highly innovative writing. With Leslie Scalapino and Michael Rothenberg, Norman serves as one of Philip Whalen's literary executors. Of late he has co-directed programs on Dharma & Diversity with Ralph Steele. His nine volumes of poetry include *On Whether Or Not To Believe In Your Mind*, and in 2004, *Slowly But Dearly* (Chax Press, Tucson). In 1998, ex nihilo press released *The Narrow Roads of Japan*, a book-length travel poem modeled loosely on the *Oku no Hosomichi* of the seventeenth century haiku master Matsuo Basho. Norman lives with his wife Kathie in Muir Beach, California, near Green Gulch, and is the father of grown twin sons.

from SUCCESS

Tuesday, 17 April

Hike to the top of Vernal Falls
As we did fourteen years before
In the rain and mist up the steep stone stairs
Now with our children who weren't then
Scampering up gleefully as we lag behind
And looking out at cliff and snow and tree
Sopping wet and amazed
The big thick Ponderosa pines
Bark all yellow-brown symmetrically scored
On the trail to Happy Isles
Such noble beings as we could never be
Quiet and massively simple
The pinkish clear forest floor so still
Not much to contend for here and not much life
Just enough
As a tributary of the Merced gushes by
This early Spring—for this place—
Where you can see the shocking redbuds all purple
And spiky in bloom
Or the bright red snowflower poking up
Among the expressionless conifers
The dogwood in bloom at exactly this moment
Some white flowers full open
And some still as tiny lively points of dazzling green
On the graceful limbs leaning at angles
To the bigger pines and firs
At the top of the Falls in the loud blasts of spray
A manzanita and a laurel low to the ground in a rock

Saturday, 1 December

Great stasis
Of Susan dead
On the bed
White and waxy
Cold flesh in the candlelight
Karen crying
Chanting sutra
Smiling to think
We all go there
For a little rest
Temporarily
Otherwise sitting all this day
Sleeping in between
Dreaming of two rooms
At the end of the line
One to the right of the bed
Dark—the one I know
One at the very end
Before the drop-off
Full of light inside
Behind the closed door
I want to enter
Though afraid
Full of world
Beyond which
Nothing
So I'm not really
Afraid at all

Monday, 3 December

During lecture garbage truck drums
Street cleaner hums
Someone thumps keys onto hardwood floor
And words, maddingly meaningless and foolish
Drone on
All heart no head
No purpose makes Jack etc.
Here in the hold or anteroom
Thoughts buzz incontrovertibly
Hard to arrest a linear progress
Of night into day or vice versa
Highly ornate statue of Monjushri
With sweet painted face
Graces my table courtesy of Jim Ryder
Can't remember
Past anymore what was
The life that went before nor can
See anywhere
The lay of the land, fence rows
Bordering fields or the main street
Where I grew up
All gone if ever there
I never saw it
Don't want to get it back
Just the wonder of the search
Finding nothing, not myself nor anyone
Not society, not history
Not the sun in the sky

FAVORABLE PROSPECTS

Resonance resplendent
Hermaphroditic puer eternal
Shooting straight up like a fountain
Running with diadems
Lives are only be stories
The body of earth ostentatious
Goaded into confused thought verities
Scooped into curette motivations
So as to merely be decisive
In conditioned ichthyic tropes
Like ichor loaves born to be mild
Income displacements
Hanging on neologistic terminologies
Spend vocabulary
Water's surface tension
Carapace so bugs can't drink stone
In the invisible worlds dangling from the testes
Clark's spelunking silence
Sphragistics gone blooey wafted vox populi

(for Clark Coolidge)

I'VE CHANGED

I've changed
Shrunk probably
Noticing the prominence of my skeleton
This word I wanted to fondle
That I threw out into the world
That never had a meaning or referent
Except to stand for all I do not know and fear
Now I can feel what it wanted to tell me

HOW THE MIGHTY HAVE FALLEN

How the mighty have fallen!
How much they have to dream about
Because what's out there's lost to them
And they dream in order to place themselves
Back inside their smoking bodies
With a scrap of paper under their tongues
A lozenge like a written remedy to keep them solid
For another day of which there are very many
That all melt into one, morning and evening
Of the first day

It's too bright in the room where you are sitting
Like a stealth kennel—time for a change
Of clothes or of scenery, time for an eclipse
Of the sun—how not being able any longer to fly
You run more recklessly up and down upon the earth
Plunge more discursively into an ocean of sound—

This is the story of people, a family
The story of a long lonely colorful dream
Of majesty and deadly proliferation
Whose cost is this sort of restraint—
The gradual creaky opening of a heavy door
Which is like a kettle, whistling
Waking you up with a start so that you blink
Looking around like a newborn babe
Or a naked grub writhing up and down
Upon the moistened earth (shatter of ashcan
Lid upon the sidewalk)—lushness on
Lushness in the half baked syntax
Of your ornery moods

Any time is breakfast time
When you've fallen into the movie time
Of memory, that careful stupid stumbling
Of a moral fugue down the doomful stairs of your pride
And hope that outruns itself in your weeping

Now that your baby is born and named
You know the terror of belonging
The responsibility of breathing plain air
Here in the diorama world
In the unadorned dismemberment of your holy temple

WHEN YOU OPEN THE GATES

When you open the gates
To speaking
Distance swallows you
The dangling words
Like columns of smoke
Ascending
Not trying to build a boat
Or threaten with a jawbone
You don't materialize as someone
Which is a relief, only the body
Like soft fur pulsing
Constantly, undulating air
Like silky water
Tumbling over a rock
Moves quiet through the mist—
Being that but not knowing it
So you could say so
Other than jabbering
Broken-open syllables
Which sound beyond intelligibility
You pass through singing

(FOR PHILIP WHALEN 1923–2002)

POETRY'S A WAY NOT A SUBJECT

Poetry's a way not a subject
In which anything appears
It's a sway among a swarm
To be hurled from side to side
Up against the language walls
That tunnel subversive
Through what is
As far as it is known
Occasioning a gap in mind
Through which you could theoretically drive a truck

Meanwhile dogs bark and canaries tweet
Monkeys propend opposable thumbs
The covering sky won't shake out its stars
To cooperate with the head's coolness
The disaster that is human life on earth—

That this can be said—that the imagination
Blisters in the cauterized night
Is possible only in the reams of paper—
These hidden significant blotches of ink
We twiddle in the dark

I know my fate rests with the splendor of diamonds—
They cannot be seen in the dark

LOTUS SUTRA

Out of the tuft of hair between his eye—
Immeasurable space filled with glowing people
Kindly preaching the Eternal Law to rapt listeners—
I had a jewel sewn into my coat, bad case of drunk
Wandering all over looking for a meal
Forgetting I was flush
Imagining I was poor
So shoveled shit among the cows for twenty years or so
Until there appears a castle in the sky
Door to which opens with a cosmic thud and a voice booms out:
"That which you now hear you already heard
That which you will later hear you hear now
And that which I should say to you
I'll never say in words only this high-pitched tone you never hear
Except in all sound the sound of silence"
Revealing that your eye's not yours and isn't dim
Your life's not yours and isn't short
But keeps on happening, blossoming
And fading as jewels, parasols, canopies, golden birdies
Every moment of every day on earth

SLIPPED AWAY

Slipped away
This occasion becomes remembering
All over again—a breath in
Then last out, final crown of a lifetime's
Utter truthfulness—
In being a person upright and tall
Noble and definite in speech
And never without a passion for what's right:
For the hopeless possible good enough world
That exists in our dreams—
Living and dying for that

(IN MEMORIUM, MAYLIE SCOTT)

SAM HAMILL has published fourteen volumes of original poetry and has translated Lao Tzu, Chuang Tzu, and most of the major poets of classical China (including Tu Fu and Li Po), Japan (Basho), and ancient Greece. He is the Founding Editor of Copper Canyon Press, situated in Port Townsend on Washington State's Olympic Peninsula. In 2003, in response to an invitation to the White House for a sedate poetry affair, he founded Poets Against the War. He delivered to Congress 13,000 poems by 12,000 poets opposing Bush's war against Iraq, and against the USA-PATRIOT act, subsequently helping establish a network of engaged poets around the world. An edited edition of *Poets Against the War* became a notable response to illicit use of American military force. Hamill is a skilled letterpress printer, regularly turning out elegant broadsides by Copper Canyon authors, and is a former book arts critic for *Bookways* and other journals. He has published three volumes of essays and edited *The Selected Poems of Thomas McGrath* and (with Brad Morrow) *The Complete Poems of Kenneth Rexroth*. He has devoted a lifetime to following a way of poetry—"'a' way because poetry is a large house with many doors which function both as entrances and as exits. No one wipes the same mirror twice." His new and selected poems and translations, *Almost Paradise*, will be published by Shambhala in March, 2005.

THE NEW YORK POEM

I sit in the dark, not brooding
exactly, not waiting for the dawn
that is just beginning, at six-twenty-one,
in gray October light behind the trees.
I sit, breathing, mind turning on its wheel.

Hayden writes, "What use is poetry
in times like these?" And I suppose
I understand when he says, "A poet
simply cannot comprehend
any meaning in such slaughter."

Nevertheless, in the grip of horror,
I turn to poetry, not prose,
to help me come to terms—
such as can be—with the lies, murders
and breathtaking hypocrisies

of those who would lead a nation
or a church. "What use is poetry?"
I sat down September twelfth,
two-thousand-one in the Common Era,
and read Rumi and kissed the ground.

And now that millions starve
in the name of holy war? Every war
is holy. It is the same pathetic story
from which we derive
"biblical proportion."

I hear Pilate's footsteps ring
on the cobblestone, the voice of Joe McCarthy
cursing in the senate, Fat Boy exploding
as the whole sky shudders.
In New York City, the crashes

and subsequent collapses
created seismic waves. To begin to speak
of the dead, of the dying… how
can a poet speak of proportion any more
at all? Yet as the old Greek said,

"We walk on the faces of the dead."
The dark fall sky grows blue.
Alone among ash and bones and ruins,
Tu Fu and Basho write the poem.
The last trace of blind rage fades

and a mute sadness settles in,
like dust, for the long, long haul. But if
I do not get up and sing,
if I do not get up and dance again,
the savages will win.

I'll kiss the sword that kills me if I must.

SEDUCING THE SPARROW

Birds live in a world without karma.
—Morris Graves

Why must the noble rose
bristle before it blooms, and why
must the frost declare
allegiance to the dew?

Don't tell me the robin's
forlorn invitation
could not be denied.
I've heard the magpie's lies.

Outside my window,
twenty-seven juncos
consort in a cedar tree,
fat and happy to be free

of all desire—ah, but
that's not true! See
how they dance and turn
when I throw out the seed.

WHAT THE WATER KNOWS

What the mouth sings, the soul must learn to forgive.
A rat's as moral as a monk in the eyes of the real world.
Still, the heart is a river
pouring from itself, a river that cannot be crossed.

It opens on a bay
and turns back upon itself as the tide comes in,
it carries the cry of the loon and the salts
of the unutterably human.

A distant eagle enters the mouth of a river
salmon no longer run and his wide wings glide
upstream until he disappears
into the nothing from which he came.

Only the thought remains. Lacking the eagle's cunning
or the wisdom of the sparrow, where shall I turn,
drowning in sorrow? Who will know what the trees know,
the spidery patience of young maple or what the willow confess?

Let me be water. The heart pours out in waves.
Listen to what the water says.
Wind, be a friend.
There's nothing I couldn't forgive.

TO HAYDEN CARRUTH ON HIS EIGHTIETH BIRTHDAY

Jesus, Hayden, it's hard to believe you're
eighty. When I began reading your work
forty years ago, how could I have known
that you were forty and forty is so young?
And how could I have ever guessed that I,
a young marine in Japan, might become
your student, your editor, your friend?

The way of poetry is mysterious,
indeed, as we discover each time we rise
into its occasion. And in the end,
it doesn't matter that we suffered or
did not suffer for our art, but that we
found in verse the courage to stand against
the state, political and religious.

How often you've said you don't know a thing
about Zen or the Tao, but you're a sage
all the same, and in the tradition of
Chuang Tzu and Confucius, a questioner,
a loner who has struggled to reach out.
And now to your Whitmanic beard, our bard
of existential grit, I raise my cup:

I wouldn't wish another eighty years
on anyone, but may you live a thousand,
and a thousand generations more. You
have shown me my way, and others their own.
You have praised what others scorned
and embraced essential *mu*, the emptiness of Zen.
Ten years ago, you wrote, "All old men are fools,"

and I thought, "Ryokan might have said that,
or maybe Yeats, or Ez in his old age,"
and laughed because it's true and getting truer
with the accumulation of my days.
You have no pride, and oh, how I admire that.
What does not change is change. Your way's my way.
In poetry, even the fool grows wise. Nine bows.

MIDSUMMER

Two yearling deer
stood in heavy falling mist
in the middle of

the road leading in-
to town, brown coats glistening,
huge eyes open wide,

caught in the headlights
in the first yellowish smear
of coming daybreak.

Twenty feet away,
I finally stopped the car
and sat still inside,

eyes locked together
in a curious searching
with those of the doe.

Minute by minute,
we were transfixed, motionless,
each imagining

the other. And then
the sun peeled back the dark clouds
like a second skin,

and, in unison,
the deer stepped slowly forward,
gently, cautiously,

off the road, into
underbrush that flourishes
along the woods' edge

and vanished in mist.
Dazed, I returned to my day,
to the work at hand.

And now, the hour late
in the morning, mist falling
again, I can still

feel my skin prickle
under those beautiful brown
doe-eyes searching me

like a lover's hand,
cautious, slowly exploring
something deep in me

I cannot touch or name.

REPLY TO T'AO CH'IEN

June rain drizzles through the heavy boughs
of cedar and spruce and knocks
the blossoms from the cherry trees.
Rhododendron blossoms also fall
as blue irises begin to open.

The bamboo shoots shoot up so quick
I can almost watch them grow.
In the first light of day I sit
in silence, watching one old crow
stalk the borders of the garden.

Whatever truth you told me
in your garden long ago,
it returns, here, now,
in the poem that begins
just beyond its words.

THE ORCHID FLOWER

Just as I wonder
whether it's going to die,
the orchid blossoms

and I can't explain why it
moves my heart, why such pleasure

comes from one small bud
on a long spindly stem, one
blood red gold flower

opening at mid-summer,
tiny, perfect in its hour.

Even to a white-
haired craggy poet, it's
purely erotic,

pistil and stamen, pollen,
dew of the world, a spoonful

of earth, and water.
Erotic because there's death
at the heart of birth,

drama in those old sunrise
prisms in wet cedar boughs,

deepest mystery
in washing evening dishes
or teasing my wife,

who grows, yes, more beautiful
because one of us will die.

JANE HIRSHFIELD

BORN IN NEW YORK CITY in 1953, Jane Hirshfield discovered Japanese haiku on her own at the age of eight, and was introduced to the practice of zazen while still in high school. She attended Princeton University, where she took courses in Chinese and Japanese literature in translation as well as poetry and first heard Gary Snyder give a talk about the Yamabushi mountain monks and his own practice of Zen. After graduating in 1973, she worked for a year on a farm, then made her way to eight years of full-time Soto Zen practice at the San Francisco Zen Center. Three of those years were spent in monastic practice at Tassajara, where Philip Whalen and Norman Fischer were her fellow students. Hirshfield received lay ordination in 1979. Featured in two Bill Moyers PBS poetry specials, *Fooling with Words* and *The Sound of Poetry*, Hirshfield has taught at the University of California, Berkeley, the University of San Francisco, Bennington College's M.F.A. Writing Seminars, and has been a visiting poet at universities around the country. She is the author of five books of poems, most recently *Given Sugar, Given Salt* (HarperCollins, 2001); a sixth will appear in early 2006. Other titles include *The October Palace* (1994) and *The Lives of the Heart* (1997), and she has published a book of Buddhist-inflected essays, *Nine Gates: Entering the Mind of Poetry* (HarperCollins, 1997). Hirshfield has also edited and co-translated two now-classic collections of poetry by women writers of the past, *Women in Praise of the Sacred: 43 Centuries of Spiritual Poetry by Women* (HarperCollins, 1994) and *The Ink Dark Moon: Poems by Komachi and Shikibu, Women of the Ancient Japanese Court* (Vintage Classics, 1990). She lives in the San Francisco Bay Area.

AGAINST CERTAINTY

There is something out in the dark that wants to correct us.
Each time I think "this," it answers "that."
Answers hard, in the heart-grammar's strictness.

If I then say "that," it too is taken away.

Between certainty and the real, an ancient enmity.
When the cat waits in the path-hedge,
no cell of her body is not waiting.
This is how she is able so completely to disappear.

I would like to enter the silence portion as she does.

To live amid the great vanishing as a cat must live,
one shadow fully at ease inside another.

THEOLOGY

If the flies did not hurry themselves to the window
they'd still die somewhere.

Other creatures choose the other dimension:
to slip
into a thicket, swim into the shaded, undercut
part of the stream.

My dog would make her tennis ball
disappear into just such a hollow,
pushing it under the water with both paws.
Then dig for it furiously, wildly, until it popped up again.

A game or a theology, I could not tell.

The flies might well prefer the dawn-ribboned mouth of a trout,
its crisp and speed,
if they could get there,
though they are not in truth that kind of fly
and preference is not given often in these matters.

A border collie's preference is to do anything entirely,
with the whole attention. This Simone Weil called prayer.
And almost always, her prayers were successful—
the tennis ball
could be summoned again to the surface.

When a friend's new pound dog, diagnosed distempered,
doctored for weeks, crawled under the porch to die, my friend crawled after,
pulled her out, said "No!",

as if to live were just a simple matter of training.

The coy-dog, startled, obeyed.
Now trots out to greet my car when I come to visit.

Only a firefly's evening blinking outside the window,
this miraculous story, but everyone hurries to believe it.

LIGHTHOUSE

Most lights are made to see by,
this to be seen.
Its vision sweeps its one path
like an aged monk raking a garden,
his question long ago answered or moved on.
Far off, night grazing horses,
breath scented with oatgrass and fennel,
step through it, disappear, step through it, disappear.

READING CHINESE POETRY BEFORE DAWN

Sleepless again,
I get up.
A cold rain
beats at the windows.
Holding my coffee,
I ponder Tu Fu's
overturned wine glass.
At his window, snow,
twelve hundred years fallen;
under his hand,
black ink not yet dry.
"Letters are useless."
The poet is old, alone,
his woodstove is empty.
The fame of centuries
casts off no heat.
In his verse, I know,
is a discipline
lost to translation;
here, only the blizzard remains.

STUDYING WU WEI, MUIR BEACH

There are days when you go
out into the bright spring fields
with the blue halter, the thick length
of rope with its sky-and-cloud braiding,
even the bucket of grain—
all corn-and-molasses sweetness,
the *maraca* sound of shaken seduction—
and the one you have gone for simply will not be caught.
It could be that the grass that day is too ripe.
It could be the mare who comes over, jutting her body
between his and yours. It could be
the wild-anise breeze that wanders in and out of his mane.
He might nip at the smallest mouthful,
but your hands' slightest rising—no matter how slow,
how cautious—breaks him away.
He doesn't have to run, though he knows he could.
Knows he is faster, stronger, less tied.
He knows he can take you or leave you in the dust.
But set aside purpose, leave the buckles and clasps
of intention draped over the fence, come forward
with both hands fully exposed, and he greedily eats.
Allows you to fondle his ears, scratch his neck, pull out
the broken half-carrot his soft-folded lips accept
tenderly from your palm. The mare edges close, and he
lays back one ear; the other stays pricked toward you,
in utmost attention. Whatever you came for,
this is what you will get: at best, a tempered affection
while red-tails circle and lupine shifts in the wind.
It is hard not to want to coerce a world that
takes what it pleases and walks away, but *Do not-doing,*
proposed Lao-tsu—and this horse. Today the world is tired.
It wants to lie down in green grass and stain its grey shoulders.

It wants to be left to study the non-human field,
to hold its own hungers, not yours, between its teeth.
Not words, but the sweetness of fennel. Not thought,
but the placid rituals of horse-dung and flies.
Nuzzling the festive altars from plantain to mustard,
from budded thistle to bent-stemmed rye. Feasting and flowering
and sleeping in every muscle, every muzzle, every bone it has.

THE DEAD DO NOT WANT US DEAD

The dead do not want us dead;
such petty errors are left for the living.
Nor do they want our mourning.
No gift to them—not rage, not weeping.
Return one of them, any one of them, to the earth,
and look: such foolish skipping,
such telling of bad jokes, such feasting!
Even a cucumber, even a single anise seed: feasting.

SEPTEMBER 15, 2001

INSPIRATION

Think of those Chinese monks' tales:
years of struggling
in the zendo, then the clink,
while sweeping up, of stone on stone . . .
It's Emily's wisdom: Truth in Circuit lies.
Or see Grant's "Common Birds And How To Know Them"
(New York: Scribner's, 1901):
"The approach must be by detour,
advantage taken of rock, tree, mound, and brush,
but if without success this way, use artifice,
throw off all stealth's appearance, watchfulness,
look guileless, a loiterer, purposeless,
stroll on (not too directly toward the bird),
avoiding any gaze too steadfast;
or failing still in this, give voice to sundry whistles,
chirp: your quarry may stay on to answer."
More briefly, try; but stymied, give it up, do something else.
Leave the untrappable thought, go walking,
ideas buzz the air like flies; return to work,
a fox trots by—not Hughes's sharp-stinking thought-fox
but quite real, outside the window,
with cream-dipped tail and red-fire legs doused watery brown;
emerges from the wood's dark margin, stopping all thinking,
and briefly squats (not fox, but vixen), then moves along
and out of sight. "Enlightenment," wrote one master,
"is an accident, though certain efforts make you accident-prone."
The rest slants fox-like, in and out of stones.

AFTER LONG SILENCE

Politeness fades,

a small anchovy gleam
leaving the upturned pot in the dishrack
after the moon has wandered out of the window.

One of the late freedoms, there in the dark.
The left-over soup put away as well.

Distinctions matter. Whether a goat's
quiet face should be called noble
or indifferent. The difference between a right rigor and pride.

The untranslatable thought must be the most precise.

Yet words are not the end of thought, they are where it begins.

RECALLING A SUNG DYNASTY LANDSCAPE

Palest wash of stone-rubbed ink
leaves open the moon: unpainted circle,
how does it raise so much light?
Below, the mountains
lose themselves in dreaming
a single, thatch-roofed hut.
Not that the hut lends meaning
to the mountains or the moon—
it is a place to rest the eye after much traveling,
is all.
And the heart, unscrolled,
is comforted by such small things:
a cup of green tea rescues us, grows deep and large,
a lake.

WHY BODHIDHARMA WENT TO HOWARD JOHNSON'S

"Where is your home," the interviewer asked him.

Here.

"No, no," the interviewer said, thinking it a problem of translation,
"when you are where you actually live."

Now it was his turn to think, *perhaps the translation?*

A CEDARY FRAGRANCE

Even now,
decades after,
I wash my face with cold water—

Not for discipline,
nor memory,
nor the icy, awakening slap,

but to practice
choosing
to make the unwanted wanted.

LAWSON FUSAO INADA

BORN IN FRESNO, California in 1938, Lawson Inada is a *sansei*—or third generation Japanese American. His paternal grandparents were sharecroppers, his father a dentist, and his mother's father opened the Fresno Fish Store. In May of 1942 President Franklin D. Roosevelt signed Executive Order 9066, removing all persons of Japanese ancestry from the West Coast. Inada went with his family first into a detention center at the Fresno County Fairgrounds, then was relocated to the internment camp in Jerome, Arkansas. He was transferred to a camp in Colorado where he remained until World War II ended. Returning to California he attended Fresno State University where Philip Levine introduced him to poetry. He also joined the Black and Chicano Set, playing bass, his music indebted to the day's great jazz musicians. *Before the War: Poems as They Happened*, published in 1971, was the first book of poetry by an Asian American to be issued by a major publishing house. This was followed in 1978 by a volume co-authored with Garrett Hongo and Alan Lau, *The Buddha Bandits Down Highway 99*. Inada's early poems are dedicated to jazz singers and instrumentalists. Recent titles deal directly with the internment camps of World War II: *Legends from Camp* and *Drawing the Line*, both published by Coffee House. He is the editor of *Only What We Could Carry*, an anthology of the internment experience. Lawson has been on the faculty at Southern Oregon University in Ashland since 1966, and has studied with the Venerable Chhoje Rinpoche.

A HIGH-FIVE FOR I-5

*

Archaeologists have determined
that the I-5 Corridor
was originally a Power Path
with sacred Prayer Places
accessible on the side.

*

Padre Yo-Cinco
headed forth
with a mission:

Each settlement now
has its own
Taco Bell.

*

The Chinese
are still blasting
I-5 into Canada.

*

I-5 is still being
excavated in Mexico.

*

I-5 is the only structure
to have its traffic
reported from the moon.

*

At any given moment,
there is enough water

in I-5 plastic bottles
to dampen a famine.

*

At any given moment,
there are more boats
on I-5 than off Cuba.

*

At any given moment,
there is more lifestyle
on I-5 in Seattle
than there ever was in Russia.

*

At any given moment,
there are more Asians
on I-5 than others
may care to imagine.

*

At any given moment,
there are more random
acts of kindness on I-5
than in medieval times.

*

If you were to chop up I-5
and lay it side by side,
you could easily cover Europe,
not to speak of encountering
unspeakable resentment.

*

If you were to roll up I-5
you could truthfully promote
the world's largest replica
of a butterfly tongue.

*

The combined cracks of I-5
are equal to the Grand Canyon.

*

The depth of I-5
is to be respected.

*

There are more I-5 reflectors
than stars in the galaxy.

*

I-5 paint can
readily cover
rain forests.

*

I-5 dashboards emit
more radiation than
all wars combined.

*

Residents east of I-5,
to the Atlantic Ocean,
are noticeably different
from those on the other side.

*

Within a 24-hour period,
I-5 roadkill could sustain,
for life, Santa's entourage.

*

The I-5 Litter Patrol
has no chance of parole.

*

All I-5 homeless
are licensed.

*

All I-5 music
is approved.

*

With the advent
of drive-thru schooling,
the Ramp Generation
never has to leave I-5.

*

The I-5 CEO's RV
is refueled while moving.

*

A proven fact:
I-5 drivers
via mirrors
read faster
backwards.

*

If ratified,
I-5 becomes
the world's

narrowest
nation.

*

Otherwise, I-5
remains the most-
traveled Möbius strip.

*

The I-5 median strip
is a designated reservation.

*

And, yes, the buffalo
have returned to I-5.

*

Improved sensors
allow many I-5 trucks,
especially at night,
to be driven by
the visually impaired.

*

In remote stretches,
beware of I-5 hijackers
and false interchanges.

*

Coming soon:
The I-5 Channel.

*

Being tested
in the Gulf:
The I-5 Auto.

*

Almost extinct:
The I-5 Bronco.

*

Almost available:
The I-5 Franchise.

*

Already in effect:
The I-5 Interstate
Date Line.

PICKING UP STONES

Nyogen Senzaki, the erstwhile Zen teacher
(he had no degrees, didn't call himself "master"),
while interned in Wyoming
(he didn't call himself "internee" either),

went about gathering pebbles
and writing words on them—
common words, in Japanese
with a brush dipped in ink.

Then he'd return them
to their source, as best he could,
the ink would wash,
and no harm was done.

However, several residents, likewise
elderly with nothing better to do,
observed his practice
and set about collecting
the Sensei's stones.

It became a kind of game
to pass the time,
to seek and find—
like an "Eastern eggless hunt."

And even in the confines of camp,
possibilities were endless—

for Senzaki, without having to resort
to trickery, would simply
scatter his gathering,

and it was difficult to tell
which was which:

"his" pebbles, just plain pebbles,
or those which, in his hands,
had remained mute,
dictating silence . . .

And it was an amusing sight
to see these old people
shuffling about in dust,
mud, snow, sleet—
sometimes even crushing
ice with their feet—

with their eyes to the ground,
bent on pursuing the old man's path,
giving everything close inspection,
pausing occasionally
to smile, exclaim, even laugh,

and essentially going around
putting rocks in their pockets . . .

Still, as they put it,
this place was perfect for pebbles,
so rich with rounded stones,
some of which reflected
the colorful proximity of Yellowstone
itself, likewise ministered
by their government;

moreover, pebble-searching
had resulted in enlightening
arrowhead finds,
inspiring some elders
to try their hand
at chipping obsidian
in this land
where the buffalo roamed . . .

Eventually, in respectable homes,
some of those stones
assumed resting places
on special mantels and shelves—

worthless souvenirs, certainly,
of only sentimental value,
for although the rocks
may speak to some
of distant days,
like mini-milestones,

they're still just anonymous rocks
with faded words on them:

MAKE TEACHING HOUSE SCENT
GREED YOUNG SEED LEAVE
NOTHING EVERYTHING CHANGE EAST
PRAY PARENTS UNIVERSE SHINE
LISTEN RESPECT KNOWLEDGE MIND . . .

And as for Senzaki,
he died in obscurity,
an old dishwasher
with few friends,

resting, perhaps,
among headstones
in Los Angeles,

a citi-Zen, of sorts,
of the earth,

one who spoke
broken English

and wrote
on some stones

WHILE LEAVING OTHERS ALONE.

ROBERT KELLY

BORN IN BROOKLYN in 1935, Robert Kelly went to a Jesuit school, to City College of New York, did graduate studies in Medieval and Renaissance literature at Columbia, worked for several years as a translator of scientific material, then began half a century of involvement with literary magazines (*Chelsea Review*, *Trobar*, *Matter*, *Caterpillar*, *Conjunctions*). His first book, *Armed Descent*, was published in 1961. *Lapis*, his sixty-third, has just been published (Godine/Black Sparrow). In recent years he has been concerned with writing-in-collaboration with artists living (Birgit Kempker: *Scham/Shame*, 2004, and Brigitte Mahlknecht: *The Garden of Distances*, 2000) and dead (P.B. Shelley, *Mont Blanc*, 1994). Forthcoming are a long poem on the discourse of psychoanalysis, *The Language of Eden*, and a collection of essays. His main work is the daily practice of poetry. He teaches in the Writing Program at Bard College, where he lives with his wife, the translator Charlotte Mandell. Since 1982, he has been a student of Tibetan Buddhism, working in the pattern taught by Kalu Rinpoche; he and his wife are students of Lama Norlha Rinpoche, under whose direction they took part in the Vajrayana Seminary Retreat from 1996–1999, at Kagyu Thubten Choling Monastery.

THREADS, 11.

Suppose it is Achilles to be told
in some language
not London not New York
some dyslexic dialect of prose
called poetry, or poesy
they used to say, the angel said,
half mocking but half amorous
of those elegant attentions
Muses waft down on their minions,
en tout cas poetry *tout court*
and the story had to ram
for all time a bronze spear prong
through the cheek and gums and jaw of a man
who still alive would live
immortal in the hour of his death
forever after
fixed in that agony
for some purpose they knew, Muses,
while the other man their scribble-servitor
only dimly
intuited in measure,
to what end you ask, and ask again,
three thousand years you ask about this war
or any, the puzzle of it,
the bronze spear breaking his face
and taciturn Achilles leaning all his force
to drive it in, and you go on reading,
what are you looking for
in this vulture feast of words, beauty,
will you rewrite the canon
to leave out war,
baffle the Saracens with peace

or leave unsmitten the lost Amelekites
and take no vengeance
ever for some smart
you barely recall
where someone touched you
wing or gill or by the breast
just under where it is heaviest
and the satin falls away,
forgiveness?

THREADS, 12.

As if war made language and language
makes war ever after
and Heraclitus was right
to say if he did say that Homer
was a fool to pray that Strife might
perish among gods and men for if it did
how would the bowstring hold
or the Pythagorean lutenist tune his cord,
how would frail molecules hold together
or Indra's net stretch softly taut
holding all things in meaningful relation
so that this kiss, she said,
though Heraclitus admitted no caresses,
might shiver out to the end of the world
and all creation feel
the amber of its tenderness,
the Weak Force, the sacred war,
but it cannot be so, because in language
a sympathy is loosed upon the world
that makes Achilles' strong arm falter sometimes,
o god let it falter, let the intended
blow and the intended victim
never meet but chase each other round the sky
forever, not round the city walls, not in dust
the starry hero and the starry victim hurry
slipping in cow dung and the shocked
laughter of the city people
trying to live their ordinary
way through even war
let the blow dissolve in air

the way the lute's interminable harmonies
shimmer outward into silence
overtone by overtone away
and no one dies.

THREADS, 20.

Art is
what has no opposite
so how do you know
as one must know
everything that's going on
anywhere, everywhere, in the world,
art has no opposite
so this thing that is seen or made or sounded
brooks no contradiction,
does that mean it has no meaning
technically, by those philosophic rules
life is guided by
candle by candle in the Bohemian turret,
brick work clammy with river damp,
o what do you see, Dr. Dee said to Sir Edward
what do you see? and it seems that Kelly
said "It sees a language
that desires us, or is that misreading, wait,
language desires us, and it sees another language
inside language, always another one
that discovers you, or is it me,
you are its me,
there's no life left to us,
we have been spoken"
and this depression kept him
from seeing any more for hours
till the doctor took him down
to the Circassian's blonde café
to drink a smoke of that opium,
so accurate its fragrance
Turks were bringing to the city in those years,
so that one lay back upon the neat divan

and dreamed all the way to Persia
where the sky is made of blue tile
and yellow tile subdues the earth
and Sir Edward woke a morning later or a noon
ready to read the pitchy stone again
while the doctor fretted and learned Czech
phrases from the innkeeper's chaste daughter,
such expressions as The oleander's poison leaves
cast healing shadows or What time
has left undone space must conclude
or folkloric wisdom of a dubious cast
like Seven crows crying mean a day without dying,
phrases for which the doctor felt a strange gratitude
as one does at outlandish things
one never would have thought oneself
and so pressed little silver coins into the cool hands
of this quiet girl, little more than a child,
who hoped one day, after her father's inevitable death,
to become a nun with her life,
and had her whole vocabulary to use up
before the silence of the convent
closed on her and the summer stars.

A Note on This Selection

I thought a long while before choosing "Threads," and these three in particular, to represent the freedom of poetry and thought that I think we have won through to, these years, via the Buddhadharma, and to embody a few core ideas I find important about Buddhism in America.

What motivated my specific choices was, for 11 and 12, the struggle against war and western heroics, a kind of calling into question of our deep prejudice (so embodied in the canon) about the nobility of heroism and high warfare. I write this in a war time, when the greatest menace to love and life and peace is the very idea that war is conceivable, even admirable. The Dee/Kelly Thread was chosen for two reasons: a delicate (I hope) tugging on the tendrils of the Western occult traditions as they open towards mantra and private (non-churchly) vision, and more Buddhist-specifically, towards the "sleep of words" towards which the poem comes, and that the Dharma masters give us as a synonym for Liberation.

Robert Kelly

JOANNE KYGER

BORN IN 1934, Joanne Kyger grew up in Santa Barbara, California, where she attended both high school and college. She moved to San Francisco in 1957, becoming one of the notable women poets associated with the San Francisco Renaissance, which included writers, painters, and dramatists. From 1960–1964 she lived in Kyoto, Japan, with poet Gary Snyder. During this time she and Snyder traveled to India with Allen Ginsberg and Peter Orlovsky, a culturaly influential trip documented in journals by herself, Snyder, and Ginsberg. Her own *Strange Big Moon: Japan & India Journals*, a classic of poetic diary writing, came out of this period. In 1964 she moved back to San Francisco, published her first books of poetry, and continued studying Buddhism, which she'd begun in Japan. She has written a Buddhist-inspired spoof on the hermetic San Francisco poetry scene, *The Dharma Society*. Long associated with the Beat poets, the San Francisco Renaissance poets, and writers of the New York School, she is a frequent teacher at both Naropa University and San Francisco's New College. Her poems are noted for their humor, their ecological alertness, and a widely traveled curiosity, often drawing on Buddhist sources, Native American lore, or playfully adopting occult themes. In recent years she has traveled frequently through Mexico. She has published over twenty books of poetry, mostly with small presses. Recent titles include *Again: Poems 1989–2000* and *As Ever: Selected Poems*. Kyger lives in Bolinas, up the coast from San Francisco, where she has edited a weekly newsletter.

IT CERTAINLY WAS DIVINE RUNNING INTO YOU

Well, just a momentary good idea as your form

changes so often I can't catch

up to you *now*
a large hawk sitting in the loquat tree close

to the ground and then
you are thunder growl borrowed from the northern

storms on their way in a day or two and leaves
are bedding their ground around the buckeye

The little chirruping flocks

Kwan Yin Willow

new moon
has hardly seemed to grow

SEPTEMBER 25, 1990

FOR YOUR BIRTHDAY, PHILIP

& UPON THE OCCASION OF BECOMING ABBOT OF THE HARTFORD STREET ZEN CENTER. OCTOBER 10, 1991

A superabundance, an excess, a plethora of greetings
May they shower down
like baby Peony
petals — but that's spring —
Isn't it   the autumnal
Imperial Kiku
every year
thinking of the chrysanthemums
Being thought of *by* them

In the fall   here
6000 feet up it's the quaking
Aspen that turn gold
Shimmering and trembling
among the steady green
of fir mountain
Who says you can't make a pond out of a bowl?
I'd better stay and fill it up   Philip
For your Birthday   — Here!
the many branches of this light
purple chrysanthemum   You can read
from this mind
giving you on paper
the faint crisp odor
of time

A late October afternoon
and the mountains are slipped in snow
A gold leaf falls
It *is* fall
And those far off peaks shining
Pure and rare.

Boulder, Colorado
With Shiki and Han Yu
October 20, 1991

Snow fall   on   green leaves
Eye is twitching quite dreadfully
I'm going to be cool
and soften the dreadful hate
and pity I have in my heart

OCTOBER 28, 1991
BOULDER

WATCHING TV

Ahoy! Electronic nightmare . . .
You don't see many Skunks watching TV
that is, if you are watching the tube
you never get to see Skunk outside strolling
in the full moon towards the compost. Good Evening
He lifts his tail. I'm just strolling, so all is well
with the smell.

A topographical enlightenment is swooning
in the back yard. Look at the sky tonight! View
the promenade of crisp hedges today. 'The world
around us is workable' when the mind
is unfettered and away from the tube, the screen;
the eyeball engaged in a back lighted room — mind tomb.

Then full moon Skunk appears delightful
with tiny frightful screams.

JUNE 23, 1994

ON THE OTHER SIDE

On the other side of the sliding glass door
about six feet away —
the scenic deer prunes the privet
thoroughly.

Look at the black stripe around her muzzle
her confident youthful grazing

in these small patches of scrub. In olden times
the voice of the deer
'was deemed a poetic thing'
with its 'sad satiety'
Say what? To the quiet muteness facing me —
so quick to catch movement,
self conscious with beauty and food
frozen with regret
too ignorant to move away
In the slanting sun setting, still 'imagining' the quiet
muttering of contented doe feeding

Lost in old time haiku, 'three times it cried'
and was heard no more
Vanishes in the out of doors.

DECEMBER 10, 1994

I BLINKED MY EYES, LOOKED UP AND EVERYONE WAS 25 YEARS OLDER

When you're alive you get to
recognize hematite,
azurite, smoked quartz,
lovely eh?
in sticky black silk

And watch simplicity
become complex in management
'Only bow when bowed to'

Go look at the sunset
Inspiration for a bunch of numbers
heralding the close of the Xian calendar
and new age metaphysical smoothies

Suddenly, I looked up, and everyone had white hair
People go in and out of your life, and your life
is a room filled with flowers and a kitchen cooking supper
and you have wrested the inscrutable from the obvious

or the other way around

We are called the exquisite bloom of February
We are called wild and grow freely

Very very annoying are people who arrive
an hour and a half late for lunch.

March 1995

"REPLACEMENT BUDDHAS"

The altar of Buddha is dark
The room has been taken
by the dolls.

—Gyodai

What do all those Buddhas *mean*
at the museum, brought from elsewhere?

Rhetorically, What do these apparitions signify?

"A magician mutters a spell over stones
and pieces of wood and produces the illusion"

of Buddhas and humans and animals and houses
"which although they do not exist in reality

seem to do so." And some people blinded
by this magical hokum-pokum

hanker after what they see — The Buddhas and fast
cars, race horses and glamorous people —

forgetting they are just stones & bones
pieces of wood

Translucent like last night's dream

From *The Life of Naropa*
March 18, 1995

WIDE MIND

Occupies a wide mind, a wide consciousness,
front page, editorial page
The winds of spring are cold and keen from the sea
Can one bring dead people to dinner?
Constantly opening up those dark arms
'I'm having a ball
sleeping with my skeleton' Allen
before he dies

A harsh hawk-like call from the cypress hedge entrance
come out come out! I am I am never
been here before See me? Stellar Stellar

Jay jaunty blue black

'Do you suppose it's him?'
'I was thinking the same thing.'

Day after A.G.'s passing
Sunday
April 6, 1997

"THE DEW SWEET LAW"

The dew sweet law
    is not flowing
      literature
          but is still

Open morning
    after morning
        and totally excellent

As the bachelor quail looks up
  in the quiet air

      all the food is his

July 23, 1998
Reading about
Nagarjuna

'RETIREMENT'

An unfamiliar warble   9 times more

cautious and deliberate   a public sound
in today's chapter of life
and nameless unless I run for the binoculars
and bird book
which I cannot because I am busy

positing thoughts in this or that direction

'against a cage of space' and reading
The New Yorker, utmost voyeurism
from a semi country life of retirement

Whoa
what a toss up
for expanded consciousness
that refuses to garden

very much but loves to fuss
and prune with the mythology
of under and   over tones

MAY 3, 2000

ONCE AGAIN ANOTHER CENTURY AHEAD

Again.   Is this happening again?
This is the thrill of a lifetime
    once more.

Continual Conscious Compassion.

Does this include even what you don't like?
    Oh ick.

DECEMBER, 2000

TO LIVE IN THIS WORLD AGAIN

You must hide yourself
change your flamboyance
to a dull hue

DOES THIS MEAN I'LL NEVER HAVE ANY FUN?

No one will notice you
The gods won't drag you off
the earth for their own

Entertainment.   You are camouflaged
with simplicity

2000

MICHAEL MCCLURE

BORN 1932 in Marysville, Kansas, Michael McClure grew up in Seattle and Wichita, attended the University of Arizona at Tucson, then settled in San Francisco. Along with Allen Ginsberg, Gary Snyder, and Philip Whalen, he read at the Six Gallery reading in 1955 memorialized in Kerouac's *The Dharma Bums* as the event that sparked the San Francisco Renaissance. McClure's poetry is grounded in both visceral and visionary approaches to the natural world—his early collection of essays is titled *Meat Science Essays*—and his poems have a distinctly biomorphic appearance on the page. Associated with the Beat poets, his writings are also in direct alignment with the mythic soundings of Blake and Shelley. In *Ghost Tantras* McClure pioneered "beast language," which extended the oral-based poetry of the 1950s by intermixing recognizable words, phrases, and lines with a range of non-sensical vocal sounds: growls, roars, coos, barks, whimpers, and moans. A prolific playwright, McClure with his cast was subject to numerous police raids in 1960s California for "obscenity" due to scenes in his underground classic *The Beard*. In recent years he has toured and performed his poetry to the accompaniment of Ray Manzarek, former keyboard player for the rock band The Doors. Early poetry titles include the sexually explicit *Dark Brown*, the celebratory "Peyote Poem," and *Hymns to St. Geryon*. Among many recent titles is the collection of Zen-inspired prayer-poems from his Oakland hills zendo, *Touching the Edge: Dharma Devotions from the Hummingbird Sangha*, with its scroll-like poems unrolling down the page.

from PLUM STONES (SEVEN/FOURTEEN/FIFTEEN)

SEVEN

BIG DUMB ANIMAL STATES.
EYES. EARS. NOSE. LOVE. HATE.
REALMS OF BLUE VELVET.
ALL IS SURFACE.
THE MIND-HEART IS DEEP.
DANCING WITH SHAPES
STEALING SELVES.
(REFINEMENTS
OF KISS
AND CLAW
FISHED
FROM
THE RIVER)
Lids half-shut.
Buttercups close to the noise
of the creek.
Mauve "shooting stars"
with white and black faces
bend over sun cups.

BIG

DUMB

ANIMAL

STATES

•

SPLOTS OF BLOOD
on asphalt
by a burst of gray feathers.
Simple stares of obvious deceit.
Pleasure in triumph.
Hair every
which
way.

•

SOCIAL
NATURE
in
boxes

•

ANIMAL STATES
real
in
vacancy.

•

V
A
C
A
N
C
Y

REAL
IN
ANIMAL STATES.

Sheer joy of swimming
around
in
the
infinite.
Space between dendrites.
Floating in nothing.
Nowhere is a place
when even dada fails.

BRIGHT SEATED FIGURE,
on your lion throne,
LET
ME
ENTER
a paradise of joy and pain
in
EACH
SUPER CLUSTER
OF GALAXIES
at
the
tip

of
a

HAIR
ON
the
SKIN
of
A
GROWING
ORANGE
CARROT,
and be your cat
who smiles from the stone wall.
—Better yet,
compassion, kindness,
and an ordinary
drop of wisdom . . .

FOURTEEN

BEDRAGGLED. GLAMOROUS. OLD AS COYOTE BREATH,
NEW AS *COMME DES GARÇONS*. HERE. GONE.
HERE. PAST SEA WORLD DRIVE.
EVEN DADA FAILED.
SMOG. BUSH POPPIES. MOUNTAIN
A
I
R
RUSTLE OF THE BLACK RIVER
MOVING WHITE STONES
WITHOUT FAIL.
LEGS CROSSED,
H
A
N
D
S
in a mudra.
SWEETNESS AND CHEERY
BLANDNESS
OF DOMESTICATION
IS
NOT
THE
WAY
to the eye of the dharma.
ALSO OUTRAGE LOSES.
I am dressed
in a robe
of
anger

sitting in an inside
no different
from outside

•

Now the sky
has
fedex planes
and stars and two planets.
AS
UNREAL
AS
MOLECULES,
STRING THEORY,
and swathed dimensions.

The robe
flashes
wizard moons,
volcanoes,
and moth jeweled
patches.

It's
B
E
T
T
E
R

to practice
seeing the mountain
and the roadside culvert
are present and gone.
NOT BLOWN OUT
like a candle,
NOT COLLAPSED
by indifference,
but they stand
on the same
feet.

•

Gassho to all sutras
Gassho to daydream cartoons
of monkey mind.
G
A
S
S
H
O
to the old scholar
surrounded
by cool snakes.

See, the landscape
of industrial buildings
(artifice of concrete)
is *THERE*
NOT THERE
THERE

THERE AND NOT THERE.

NEARBYE
are the foot prints of mastodons
and camel herds in pleistocene earth.
Real
and
solid
as
a
flea
market

FIFTEEN

WELCOME DEAR CHAOS.
WELCOME LIGHT
OF THE ROAR.
CALM LIGHT OF THE ROAR.
SOUND OF A FEATHER
FALLING
IN SOME PARADISE.
PARADISE NEARBYE.

R
O
A
R

L
I
G
H
T
in
ordinary
BLACKNESS.

TRANSPARENT
B
L
A
C
K
N
E
S
S

ZINGS
out and in.

Sculptured hands
of a seated figure.
Half-closed eyes.
Plain as disturbance and straw
and Grandpa's tin snuff box.

NO LIGHT

NO STRAW

NO DONKEY

Even dada failed.

The sutra rests on a lotus.
One hand swings the sword.
Flame edges are blades,
chopping out walls
freeing the realms.
Serious as comedy.
CARTOONS OF NO HEAVEN.
Where is a beginning or end?
Tied up string and star cliffs?
No beginning or end.

Cartoons of no heaven.
Straw and Grandpa's snuff box.
The mind in the hands knows.
HERE.
Six trillionths of a moment.

Sometimes a Stan Brakhage film
projected on the skin
of a tadpole;
more
often
WISDOM
DISGUISED
AS
COMPASSION.

Roaring in the four corners.
The center is unutterably calm,
and does not seem so
before birth flashes
lightening and turquoise.
We sit on black cushions
in
the
C
O
L
D
N
E
S
S

THOREAU'S EYES

TWO POEMS FOR KAZUAKI TANAHASHI

one

REVEL IN THE CONTRADICTIONS OF LOVE AND PAIN
AND DEEP THOUGHT.
Thoreau's eyes are there to thank you a lot
for the courage to bear the curse
and laugh at the actions you make in your stealth.
In Thoreau's worn eyes is a glory of health.
We are part sweatly stallion and part opalescent elf —
AND
IT
IS
ALL
O.K.
as a long-gone childhood pouring forth the odor of hay

two

"REMAINING UNBLEMISHED BY THE DUST OF SENSATION
IS GUARDING THE DHARMA,"
forget life and death, birth, escape and karma.
The smell of creamy carnations
SETS
YOU
FREE
for mind and body to flee
forward to the stream that flows from the sea
into a statue that breathes
above your crossed legs and knees.
Each blotch on the snake is perfect.
In sight, sound, taste, touch and smell
there's no defect
no hell
not
even
nothing.

UNCHANGED

NO MEAT, NO MIND, NO CONSCIOUSNESS,
NO ONE TO BE FREE OF DARKNESS
OR FOR THE LIGHT TO FIND IN UNIVERSES OF WHITE EAGLE
WINGS—WHERE I HAVE BEEN WITH YOU!
With no regret we will leave
as if we
WERE NEVER HERE
holding it precious and perfect
IN THE ONGOING NOTHINGNESS

((^^^^
^^^^^^^^^^^))

BORN AND UNBORN, TASTES OF DARK CHOCOLATE,
touch of lavender cashmere,
NOT EVEN KNOWING
there's nothing
to
forget

—even tired arm muscles after swimming.

THIS IS OUR PERFECTION

from TOUCHING THE EDGE: DHARMA DEVOTIONS

FROM THE HUMMINGBIRD SANGHA (FOUR POEMS, 34, 46, 98, 99)

34

TO GIVE IS THE WHITE HAND
with the long fingers
and the eye in the palm
P
U
T
T
I
N
G
FORTH
what is one,
already arisen,
and long gone.

The squawking of jays
is
a gift in the trees.
BE IN COMFORT CHET BAKER.
BE IN COMFORT JEAN-MICHEL BASQUIAT.

There are waves
and facets
and overlappings
and slidings
of
chunks
(and
non-chunks)

slipping
into
the ordinary
E
M
P
T
Y
roar
of the lion.
Plain
as
consciousness.

NOT THERE

46

THE CALICO CAT LIES
on the high ledge
in the darkness
feeling
the huge space,
blinking
at light
in the crack
under the door.
— IT'S JUST
THE SAME
WITH ME;
I
imagine
a shudder of pleasure
and
the sense
of something
beyond self
filling emptiness
among cartons of old books,
a stored
vanity table,
and an antique sewing
machine
HOW
PERFECT
and
MOMENTARY
and
ETERNAL

Remember
pollywogs in cold
spring ponds

and

their
big

dark eyes

98

SILENCE IS A ROAR
with white hands.
NOISE
is born out
of it
distracting me
with the purple arms
of mexican sage.

Sun
slips into this realm
with a psychedelic flash.
I
find a grain
of compassion
and its polished surface
mirrors my face.
THIS
IS
ME
AS
I AM.

SEE
MY
EYES
AND
MY NOSE
and my mouth

ME

AS

I
AM

reflected from pearl
to pearl
in the crown

99

DARK PATHS ARE THE WAY
to the light
in
the
forest
where the mountain gleams
after rain
and thunder.
S
E
L
F
KNOWLEDGE
flashes like sun
in a downpour.
A
milligram
is
PURE
GOLD
wrapped in actions
and carried to the old boat.
The rustlings of leaves
in the yard are songs
of clarity
praising the changing
of forms.

We are the touch of silk
and taste of peaches and steamed beats.

HOW SOLID AND EMPTY.

HOW

SOLID

AND

EMPTY

IS

THIS

DHARMA

from HAIKU ROWS

for Diane di Prima

AROUND
THE
EARS
a puff
of
cherry blossom smell

for Jack Kerouac

NOT SNOW
BUT
a plum petal
falling
before
thunder
starts

for Gary Snyder and Carole Koda

((AHH! A TINY
SEA LION VOICE
in wave-mountains
of groans and roars))

for Marilyn and Stan Brakhage

SILVER OCELOT
S
P
O
T
S
race
past
the crescent moon.

Car door slams.

for Zenshin Ryufu Philip Whalen

In the lion's eye
THE BLACK CUSHION
is
compassion.

HARRYETTE MULLEN

HARRYETTE MULLEN is the author of six poetry books: *Tree Tall Woman, Trimmings, S*PeRM**K*T, Muse & Drudge, Blues Baby*, and *Sleeping with the Dictionary*, a finalist for the National Book Award, Los Angeles Times Book Prize, and National Book Critics Circle Award. Her work has been widely published in periodicals and anthologies, including a recent edition of the *Norton Anthology of African American Literature*. Her honors include a fellowship from the Society for the Humanities at Cornell University and a Rockefeller Fellowship at the Susan B. Anthony Institute at University of Rochester, as well as artist residencies awarded by the Texas Institute of Letters, the Helene Wurlitzer Foundation of New Mexico, and the Virginia Center for Creative Arts. She has taught at Cornell University and currently holds a joint appointment in English and African American Studies at UCLA. Mullen was born in Florence, Alabama, birthplace of blues legend W.C. Handy. She grew up in Fort Worth, Texas, home of jazz innovator Ornette Coleman. Mullen's family roots are in Virginia, Pennsylvania, Alabama, and Texas. One of her African-American ancestors, a Union soldier, was at Appomattox when Lee surrendered to Grant. Another early black relative, a former slave from Alabama, served in the Texas Legislature during Reconstruction.

SOUVENIR FROM ANYWHERE

People of color untie-dyed. Got nothing to lose but your CPT-shirts. You're all just a box of crayons. The whole ball of wax would make a lovely decorator candle on a Day of the Dead Santeria Petro Vodou altar. Or how about these yin-yang ear-rings to balance your energy? This rainbow crystal necklace, so good for unblocking your chi and opening the chakras? Hey, you broke it, you bought it! No checks accepted. Unattended children will be sold as slaves.

MANTRA FOR A CLASSLESS SOCIETY, OR MR. ROGET'S NEIGHBORHOOD

cozy comfortable homey homelike
sheltered protected private concealed covered
snug content relaxed restful sedate
untroubled complacent placid serene calm undisturbed
wealthy affluent prosperous substantial
acceptable satisfied satisfactory adequate
uncomfortable uneasy restless
unsuitable indigent
bothersome irritating painful
troublesome discomfiting disturbing
destitute impoverished needy
penniless penurious poor
poverty-stricken embarrassing
upsetting awkward ill-at-ease
nervous self-conscious tense

XENOPHOBIC NIGHTMARE IN A FOREIGN LANGUAGE

WAKING UP WITH ENRIQUE CHAGOYA

Whereas, in the opinion of the Government of the United States the coming of bitter labor to this country endangers the good order of certain localities within the territory thereof:

Therefore, be it enacted by the Senate and House of Representatives of the United States of America in Congress assembled,

That from and after the expiration of ninety days next after the passage of this act, and until the expiration of ten years next after the passage of this act, the coming of bitter labor to the United States be, and the same is hereby, suspended; and during such suspension it shall not be lawful for any bitter labor to come, or, having so come after the expiration of said ninety days, to remain within the United States.

That the master of any vessel who shall knowingly bring within the United States on such vessel, and land or permit to be landed, any bitter labor, from any foreign port of place, shall be deemed guilty of a misdemeanor, and on conviction thereof shall be punished by a fine of not more than five hundred dollars for each and every such bitter labor so brought, and may be also imprisoned for a term not exceeding one year.

That any person who shall knowingly bring into or cause to be brought into the United States by land, or who shall knowingly aid or abet the same, or aid or abet the landing in the United States from any vessel of any bitter labor not lawfully entitled to enter the United States, shall be deemed guilty of a misdemeanor, and shall, on conviction thereof, be fined in a sum not exceeding one thousand dollars, and imprisoned for a term not exceeding one year.

That no bitter labor shall be permitted to enter the United States by land without producing to the proper officer of customs the certificate in this act required of bitter labor seeking to land from a vessel. And any bitter labor found unlawfully within the United States shall be caused to be removed therefrom to the country from whence they came, by direction of the United States, after being brought before some justice, judge, or commissioner of a court of the United States and found to be not lawfully entitled to be or remain in the United States.

May 6, 1882

ZEN ACORN

FOR BOB KAUFMAN

a frozen
indian acorn

a frozen
indiana corn

afro zen
indian acorn

afro zen
indiana corn

a zen fro
in diana corn

frozen fan
in zero canadian

indian corn for
arizona nonradiance

a narco dozen
faze an african

KAMASUTRA SUTRA

This is a story I have heard:

Entwined in a passionate embrace
with his beloved wife,
the holy one exclaimed,
"I have reached enlightenment!"

His devoted partner responded,
"I'm truly happy for you, my love,
and if you can give me another minute,
I believe I'll get there too."

HOA NGUYEN

HOA NGUYEN was born January 26, 1967, near Saigon. At 18 months of age she moved to the United States and was raised in the Washington, D.C., area. She studied poetry in San Francisco, remained active in the Bay Area writing scene for several years, and currently lives in Austin, Texas, with her husband, the poet Dale Smith, and their two children, Keaton and Waylon. Together she and Dale edit *Skanky Possum*, a small press poetry journal that features individually stamped and stenciled covers as well as a radically independent approach to contemporary verse. *Skanky Possum* is also a book-publishing imprint and a web site that features poetry and reviews of small press books. Hoa teaches creative writing in various settings to both youths and adults, and leads an online workshop through Teachers & Writers in New York City. She writes in a letter, "My mother was raised Buddhist but was a non-practicing adult. Buddhism as a practice / body of thought was something I had to recover as an adult, which also coincided with my study of poetry / practice. I think of myself as Buddhist at least in thought / life approach but don't feel I can claim myself as a Buddhist since I have no formal sitting practice." In 2002, the subpress collective published her first book-length collection, *Your Ancient See Through*, with drawings by Philip Trussell, the source for the selection of poems included here.

[BUDDHA'S EARS ARE DROOPY TOUCH HIS SHOULDERS]

Buddha's ears are droopy touch his shoulders
as scarves fly out of windows and I shriek
at the lotus of enlightenment

Travel to Free Street past Waco
to the hole in the Earth
wearing water

I'm aiming my mouth
for apple pie

LOZENGE

There's a revolution going on
and commercials & football on TV
Secret
river in the sky   it's a tree or crocodile
Mayans say it ends in 12 years
(sky fall down)

layer   layer   layer

I could be born graceful
to pull turnips or rice
or tricks all my life
long wavy hair   plump lips

and then die
The secret seed of the thing

Bulbing words
throb the way hearts do

[UNORTHODOX & IMPRACTICAL ONE NOT LED]

Unorthodox & impractical one not led
easily and conceals my greed under
friendliness I am a tiger wife
a tiger in each knee like silent
pissed off Kaufman I am guilty
I am tragic I must die being
Ho Chi Minh & Groucho Marx and also
Isadora Duncan

[SITTING THERE NEARLY TRANSLUCENT YOU'LL END UP]

Sitting there nearly translucent   You'll end up
having to bury him   Higher elevations
are cold make your lips turn blue

I sat in a tree with a wire star
the kind you find at the last minute

"memories"

Poppies that fade as bright at that
rubbing plastic beads against your teeth

(inward now)

The cave the dancer made

"Flowers for ritual or medicine"

SHRED

we are complicating
patterns.   destiny

            is a big room.   we talk
like jets missing

home: a view of sky as a child
a cotton diorama.

birds collect where they will
telephone wire.   the front stoop.

what days aren't pinched by absence

we are here
in our skin.   destiny

            is a small city
I could die today.

[HOUSE ON FIRE MY MOM'S]

house on fire   my mom's
past house   a child   she
lost the tea pot shaped
from a big hard fruit
Gone too the rain
trees   how they curved
in to bring water
for store   (drink)   wash
in the river

MISSION DOLORES

Stream of our Lady of Sorrows
Dolores   though the river is gone now
            Ring your bell on holy days   sunny
Mission and the old cemetery
in the District of Missions

    Palmy Dolores
bright ceiling dim with candle smoke
survivor of earthquakes and fires
(Dolores and her gold fire hydrant)

$1 will get you history
  museum entry and a California moment
Dolores where I kissed you
  for a lifetime wishing fierceness
to die with you or maybe
                just after you

CAPTIVE AND ABLE

Bells gathered like bells   What are
captive and able   thin clapper clapping
cast in a bell   in a jealous bell

I am a gatherer in the jealous bell
the ugly tangent cast in a race
(divergently) I am so unfair

sometimes   believing the bells
and jealous of someone else

DARK

then owl
yellow-eyed   black pupil

this is a body going numb from will
meeting the outside world   forehead

where the feathers were   she blinks   Athene
how your wisdom darkens   makes

trouble for me to see in the eye's center
grapple after life's cog—anima—

special where rain is caught
on the tongue   now my left hand is

numb where the knowledge knife is gifted
and owl nimble-necked blinks at me   certain

CALM IN THE VEGETABLE BEARD OF TIME

His golden ear-loops cover
handsome honed cheek bones
with wonder   My-eyed wonder at
gazing   him   speechless   nearly
no mouthed beneath the varying
grey green blue   of his wise chin

Dots   Dots or a ladder connect us
Insect antennae   antennae under water
as in crawfish whisker carp   Speckled
forehead wrinkles at Rilke when I say "Beauty
is nothing but the beginning of terror"
Laugh   Shake your head   I saw
noses first   felt my own   the issuing
spot through which I begin and begin again

[CROWS AND GRACKLES   GRACKLES]

Crows and grackles   grackles
in the sycamore   food cruising
I'm broke and the sauce burns
I sprinkle ashes in the flowerbed
I kiss your cat

It doesn't matter that fate can't rain
and write flower again
          Want me a handsome bird
      black toenails that curve
West of Sunny's Wigs
          the goddess Gaia shaking her dirty hair

[ROLL IN YOUR SKULL GONE GREEN]

Roll in your skull gone green
like a mossy cog that wings
Sing the good times
You seem a tiny wrecked thing to me
something sacred   where time has gone
old and green   Norse
hymns bringing dawn

MIKE O'CONNOR

MIKE O'CONNOR is a poet and a translator of Chinese literature. A native son of the Olympic Peninsula, Washington State, he spent more than a decade farming in the Dungeness-Sequim River Valley and cedar-logging and tree-planting in the Olympic Mountains. From 1979 until 1995, he lived mostly in the Republic of China, Taiwan, studying Chinese language and culture while working as a journalist for Chinese news organizations. He was part of an expatriate group that included American translators Red Pine and David Hinton as well as the German translator Stefan Hyner, who have brought Chinese poetry and Buddhist literature to a new generation of Western readers. An M.F.A. graduate of the Jack Kerouac School, Naropa University, and a recipient of a literature fellowship from the National Endowment for the Arts, O'Connor currently resides with his wife Liu Ling-hui, a dance teacher and choreographer, in Port Townsend, Washington. Among his books are two volumes of translation from Wisdom Publications, *The Clouds Should Know Me by Now: Buddhist Poet-Monks of China*, edited with Red Pine (1998), and *When I Find You Again, It Will Be in Mountains: Selected Poetry of Chia Tao (779–843)*. He is the poetry editor for the alternative newspaper of the Olympic Peninsula, *Vigilance*. *When the Tiger Weeps*, a volume of poems released in 2004, is his eighth book.

KEROUAC CREEK WORK TUNE

After three days of summer rain,
I'm back splitting cedar
in the hills.
The horse skid-trail
is muddy
and rain clouds dapple
the peaks.

But work goes well,
the saw and truck run fine;
cedar splits
into fifty
sturdy rails,
and by evening
—truck loaded, tools packed away—

the moon and stars
jingle in the sky
like wages.

KUAN-YIN SHAN: MOTHER-OF-MERCY MOUNTAIN

We also like blown cloud
across the face of the mountain . . .
An old woman cooking
noodles for young soldiers
in a makeshift wooden lean-to. A nice
fire

while fog-swirls dampen our sweaters.

The summit's not far, a stone's throw to the stone marker
clear of razor grass (*mang t'sao*) and cloud. And east
in descending veils: the rain—where the Strait should
be—then all the rest of China.

Kuan-yin, Bodhisattva of Compassion,
Kuan Shih-yin, Hearer of Cries; when
in trouble, she heals without question,
no credentials required.
Office hours: Eternal.

The washed-out rocky path
drops quickly; grass arches over
our heads. The path becomes trail
through bamboo and mulberry,
becomes road past tea farms
and grave sites,
rock quarries and oranges,

descending to the ferry town Pa-li,
where the water of the Tamsui broadens
before sweeping to the sea.

At the ferry landing, a shack
on pilings pours forth a smoke
black as the sand they're
sucking from the river bottom
and dumping in the bucket of a Cat.

> Then the river ferry comes,
> low in the rainbow oily water
> that reflects Kuan-yin.

ON THE ROAD TO DENVER IN A COAT AND TIE, I THINK OF MY OLD FRIEND MASTER RED PINE AND THE EXAMPLE HE INSPIRES

You had to stop giving blood
for a living, it was killing you
in a different way than ordinary work.

"Hey, all I want to do," you always said,
"is just stay up here on Yang-ming Mountain
and translate Buddhist poems.

"And take hot sulphur baths,
drink spring green tea and
have the three German girls come up on weekends
bearing gifts of Glenfiddich and sandalwood fans."

Admirable as this agenda was,
you finally had to get a job—

> (Even your sideline manuscript,
> purloined from Mimi,
> called: "White Girls in Asia,"
> languished in your lacquer desk.)

duty-running for a gang of merchants
operating out of Hongkong and Taipei.

You flew so frequently,
Cathay Airlines bestowed on you
its Marco Polo Gold

("What's that goddamn thing, Red?")

with all its perks and privileges:
access to the Marco Polo Lounge,
free drinks and implied flirtation rights
with native-costumed flight attendants.

("Hey, Red, can we see that card?")

On trips, of course, you wore
a coat and tie, which as you said
was disingenuous, but modern Chinese disguise,
and even hooked your younger brother
into flying (sort of shotgun) at your side.

Green rice-paddies near Taoyuan;
Laundry-draped balconies of high-rise Kowloon;
Neat *hinoki* woodlots near Narita;
The river fog from the Han at Kimpo—

All glimpsed from a tiny window
going into, or falling out of,
the clouds.

("Hello, Mr. Pine, so good to see you again,
your room is 405; my, that's a beautiful
arm of watches, Mr. Pine.")

The duty-runner:

Your bags stuffed with nylons, dresses,
the latest hand-held instruments, toys,
electronic devices, gizmos, gimcracks,
chocolates, cosmetics, vitamins,
shoes, oil-paper parasols and saki.

And yes, the Rolex watches

wearing hairless and smooth the skin
on your left arm.

A technically not illegal end-run
(except, perhaps, for the watches)
around government Customs
to bring cheaper goods
to all the yearning markets of Asia's
teeming tariff-burdened folk;

Our border-opening hero:
("Here little Wang, a toy from Hongkong.")
Our jet-age Robin Hood:
("This tape will self-destruct . . .")
And a whole bag of tricks
& monkeyshine, off-the-cuffs, up-the-sleeves,
under-the-tables, now-you-see-its, now-you-don'ts,
hair-raising, white-knuckle adventures and escapes
in the Kafkaesque ports of entry,
in the tidal confluence of commerce and thieves.

Just to get back
to a cup of fragrant tea
and the four-line songs
of Cold Mountain—Han Shan—

who wiped his hands of the "red dust"
more than a thousand years ago
for a thatched hut,
some peace of mind,
and the immortal mists
of the Heavenly Terrace Mountains,

and wrote:

> "You're all a band of angels
> in a leaking boat at sea."

SOLILOQUY OF THE DANISH CLOISTER

"What's the Latin word for parsley?"
"What's the Greek name for Swine's Snout?"

—Robert Browning,
"Soliloquy of the Spanish Cloister"

After evening sitting,
Brother Joe confides,
"My legs were killing me
that time, waiting for the bell."
I'm lending Joe some art books
so he can paint a Buddha on the zendo wall.
I flip to a plate of the colossal Buddha,
cave XX, Yun-kang, Shansi.
"Yeah?," he says.

Brother Steve, in beard and wild hair,
joins us, saying, "Man, I just couldn't quit thinking
of how to hang that show."
He's a photographer and I've thrown in a few pictures of Japan
to go with his exhibit at the Salal Cafe.
"Yes," I say. "I thought a little of the show myself;
but then decided to let you think about it."

Soon, Abbot Niels, the Dane, shows up
and leads us where he plans to build—
completely out of rubbish—a cabin.
"Of course, I'll push a little beyond the building code," he says
"and then play absolutely dumb."
He laughs and hops about and rolls another
American Spirit cigarette.

When he's arrested,
I figure I'm the leading candidate for roshi.

Sitting Frog Zendo Port Townsend April 30, 1999

SAKURA

Lingering at the door of the bathhouse,
I watch the woman bundle off children
into light-rain, small-lane Kyoto.

Skirt in hand, she glances
my way across the evening lane,
then up the walk after the party
of colored rain boots and umbrellas.

Wet-headed but warm, I'm waiting
for Hui to come out from the public bath,
but can't help thinking of America,
the disquietude strangers there inspire.

Cherry trees are just beginning to break
blossom, here, off Kitaoji-dori, north of town.

Now the woman is crossing the lane,
coming directly toward me. She wants
to give me her open umbrella,
insists that I take it

without knowing where I'm going
or who in the world I am.

I thank her and bow,
and point to my broadbrimmed hat.

Am I sure, she implores, am I sure?

There's hardly a raindrop
in the rain-sweetened air.

She smiles and bows,
returns to the sliding doors of her house.

Kyoto, the old capital,
bursts into blossom in my heart.

SHIN YU PAI

SHIN YU PAI was born in the American Midwest, year of the wood rabbit, September 28, 1975, the same birthday as Confucius. A poet, photographer, and book artist, she grew up in Southern California, then went east for college. At Boston University she embarked on the study of Eastern religions and Buddhism with M. David Eckel who introduced her to the texts of Ryokan and Milarepa. She continued her education at The Naropa Institute—"an isolating, strange and wonderful place"—where she studied, among other things, Japanese tea, meditation, and translation. She completed her interdisciplinary studies at the Art Institute of Chicago in 1999 and has been a practicing poet and photographer since. Of her background she says: "Buddhism provides me with the framework that has always been part of my experience, growing up as a child of Taiwanese immigrants. Religion for my family was highly syncretic and socialized, a blending of Taoist, Buddhist, Confucian, and folk beliefs that was impossible to articulate." Shin Yu has a chapbook of translations from classical Chinese verse, *Ten Thousand Miles of Mountains and Rivers*, and her photography has been exhibited throughout the Midwest. A collection of poetry, *Equivalence*, appeared in 2003, from which the poems in this collection are drawn. She lives in Dallas, Texas.

YES YOKO ONO

一

Stones

Remove a stone from an unmarked pile.
Choose one pile to add it to—
a mound of joy
or a mound of sorrow.
Or take a stone from a mound of sorrow
and move it to a mound of joy.

二

Painting to let the evening light come through

Lift the blind of the bedroom window.
Place a clear glass bottle
on the window sill.
The painting exists when
the stars have risen.

Painting for the wind

Write down your favorite words
on separate scraps of paper.
Leave the paper where there is wind.
The scraps of paper can be lottery receipts,
business cards, or paper napkins.

四

Painting to hammer a nail

Hammer a nail into a mirror.
Place the pieces
in an abandoned lot
with an unobstructed view of
the sky.

五

PAINTING TO BE CONSTRUCTED IN YOUR HEAD

Imagine a painting.
Cut out colors, shapes, and things you like.
Paste them on a blank background.
Cover the whole thing in a wash of white,
or whatever is your favorite color.

Sheep piece

Borrow a herd of sheep,
one hundred in number or more
spray paint their fleece
with your favorite words.
Watch from a distance as the sheep
arrange themselves into poems.

七

Housecleaning piece

Remove all the light
bulbs from the fixtures.
When night has fallen
organize your things
into boxes.

THE GATHERING AT THE ORCHID PAVILION

Entering a darkened room
to pass between sixteen pillars
of equal height and depth,
ten feet high and one foot square,

I place my hand against the grain
hold my ear to a pillar
listening for something
like the sound of trees.

Across the room
six folded screens
colored ink and gold on silk

the specks of turquoise in those mountains
glimmering points of light
from a distance
the shine of moss

in memory like the lights
of houses in the hillsides
lanterns in the sea
of winter nights.

Mist erases crags and peaks.

Bearded scholars on blankets
read to one another
calligraphing poems
under shade of bamboo and plum

as servants fill cups
with rice wine
floated downstream
on lotus pads.

My breath clouds the casing
as I think of humidity
and the desire to touch things.

The door of the gallery opens.
A father and his daughter

I think we've seen this one before, the girl says.
They look for the place where the story begins.
The girl kisses the glass.

Where does the story begin?
Father insists gently.

In the mountains, the girl cries.

Traces of handprints left on the glass.

It starts here, she says
Here.

OFFICE FENG SHUI

A specialist is brought in to the Buddhist college to redirect the negative energy flowing from the tail of the dragon through Arapahoe Avenue, and into the corner suite of the main office. He rearranges the furniture, and everything red is removed. Red, the color of padma, manifests as passion in its neurotic state and draws out the existing energy in a field. The staff member in the room closest to the street is removed from her office, which has been marked with two 2's, the number of disease. ($2 + 2 = 4$, the Chinese number of death. But not quite that serious, according to the specialist.) He prescribes fish. Fish, the symbol for prosperity and good luck, will absorb the negativity. Since real fish would die in the windowsill, the specialist brings in a miniature tank of hand-painted magnetic fish. The bands of orange and red on the fish have been carefully concealed with blue and yellow acrylic paint. To maintain fake fish: Reach a hand into the aquarium when the fish stop swimming and clump together, grab the fish by their tails, and shake the bubbles from their bodies.

FRUIT THEY HAD IN COMMON

He was convinced that you had to eat the entire thing in one sitting. A condition of childhood and a grandmother who served watermelon to the grandchildren entrusted to her care, as meal (breakfast, lunch, *and* dinner), in between her requests of stirred martinis and service in bed. He remembers reading a haiku by a Japanese poet in which a farmer invokes a spell upon his watermelon patch. When thieves approach at night to steal the fruit, the watermelons transform into frogs and escape. As a boy, he often wished that the watermelon on his plate would come alive and hop away.

She had her own memories of summer fruit—an ama who educated her in maintaining a balanced diet of hot and cool foods. During the hot season, Grandmother insisted she rub the white of the rind over her face until sticky and wet. She had a theory concerning cool foods and their absence in the diet of prominent government leaders—for instance, if the Chinese would only eat more carrots it would cool their ardor for conquering foreign nations and erasing history.

DALE PENDELL was born in California in 1947 into a family of teetotaling Methodists. He stuck out his thumb before he was really old enough, hoping to find a life. Instead, maybe he lost it. As Chou-En Lai remarked, when asked about his feelings on the French Revolution, "It's too soon to tell." He studied with a number of different Buddhist teachers before settling in at Ring of Bone Zendo, in the Sierra Nevada foothills, which he helped found in 1974. He still sits there on occasion, usually mistaken for a bag of rice. In the 1970s he was the editor and publisher of *Kuksu: Journal of Backcountry Writing*, and later of the *Exiled-In-America* series of chapbooks. Recent publications include *Living With Barbarians: A Few Plant Poems*, from Wild Ginger Press, and *Pharmako/Poeia* and *Pharmako/Dynamis*, the first two of three volumes of a poetic history of psychotropic plants, both from Mercury House. Hakim Bey has written, "[these volumes] will be preserved among the scriptures of an entheogenic revival that will recognize the scribe Pendell as an inspired prophet and forerunner." Dale has worked as a laborer, botanist, and computer scientist. He lives in Penn Valley, in the Sierra foothills, with his wife Laura, also a poet. Their music and performance group, Oracular Madness, appeared at Burning Man in 2004.

AMṚTA:
THE NEUROPHARMACOLOGY OF NIRVANA

Awash in chemicals: peptides and alkaloids, hormones and enzymes, pheromones, sugars, and fatty acids. Tiny neurotransmitters: nitric oxide, hydrogen sulfide, and their big buddies: phenethylamines—dopamine and epinephrine; tryptamines—serotonin and melatonin.

Feedback loops and regulators, intricate biosynthetic pathways cross-linked and interwoven, like complex food-chains in a tropical forest.

Or maybe a Precambrian sea.

Which one is us? Are endorphins compassionate, adrenaline aggressive?

We tend to emphasize the brain as the center of consciousness, imagine it to be a computer full of wires, but Aristotle was not incorrect when he recognized that the brain was a secretory gland.

All in solution. Ions dissolved in synaptic fluid,
passing through membranes—
neurotransmitters binding to receptors,
electronic keys probing macromolecular locks,

There are dozens of receptor types and subtypes known. Receptors occur throughout the body, not just the brain. There are serotonin receptors on blood platelets—the immune system like a second, decentralized brain, distinguishing "self" and "other."

The Discriminating Wisdom.

And the central nervous system is mirrored in the digestive tract: the "enteric" nervous system—one hundred million neurons embedded in the lining of the esophagus, stomach, and intestines, complete with neurotransmitters, synapses, and the ability to learn.

Cause or effect, hard to say: mood shifts change the chemistry, changing the chemistry alters mood.

We reflect the environment, permeable and penetrating, an analog-coded map. The protocol, deep down somewhere, perhaps wave equations, but the language is molecular: neurotransmitters are the lexicon, metabolic pathways the grammar.

> *Who speaks this language?*
> *We sit. Laugh. Sing.*
> *We dream.*

# # # # # # # # # # # # # # # #

Many neurotransmitters are of ancient lineage. Some of the same molecules are found in mammals and reptiles, insects and mollusks. No reason to throw out a good idea.

Some of them are also found in plants. Mostly though, like large pharmaceutical firms, plants synthesize analogs: a patented chemical that has the same functionality as its type. As plant-insect relationships are often characterized by strife as well as by love, many of these chemicals, the alkaloids especially, are poisons, usually insect poisons. They fit into the plugs and gears of some finely tuned invertebrate biosystem and monkey-wrench it.

Some plant poisons mimic neurotransmitters. And since the nervous system tends to be conservative, compared with other biological systems, these plant poisons can also mimic human neurotransmitters, or interact with human consciousness in some other way.

This is a generalization, of course. Nobody knows for sure what the plants are up to. Sometimes they spend a significant amount of their energy and resources budget on synthesizing a chemical that serves no known purpose. For the plant, anyway. For human beings, the effects of the substance can be marvelous, divine.

> *Thus bhang, Cannabis sativa, is said to have sprung up where Shiva spilled a few drips of Amrita, or Ambrosia, the heavenly drink of the gods. Other sacred plants, like the mushrooms, Psilocybe ssp., and the peyote cactus, Lophophora, are considered deific by their peoples: the gift of God, or indeed, the actual body of God.*

Sacred plants have been our companions since the Paleolithic. In those times, the scientists and healers, the poets and prophets, learned how to use these plants, and discovered deeper layers to the world, beyond its usual appearance. That what seems is not necessarily what is.

Possibly they discovered language. Certainly they discovered animism. They saw that the earth was alive, and that everything that happened or existed was connected to everything else. They discovered that sickness lay within, that the Self had an inner structure where dramatic scenes were enacted: theater, masks. That sometimes a person got lost while passing through this realm, so was a confused type of person, or lost something there, like a shadow, or playfully tried on one of the masks and forgot to take it off, and got stuck in it.

> *Some of them saw all the way to the core: these were the Paleolithic Buddhas.*

The Paleolithic plant-teaching lineage and its descendants is still alive and being practiced by many native peoples, and by a few religious sects in India and Africa. In the West, plant religions were severely persecuted, generally to extinction. A few pockets have survived, such as *Amanita muscaria* use by certain groups of rural Catalonians.

################

Buddhism, with a few possible exceptions, has mostly abandoned the use of natural substances in yogic practice, substituting instead a variety of artificial techniques.

Traces remain, hemp seeds in tantric rituals.

The reasons for the rejection of psychoactive plants may well be political as much as spiritual/practical. Buddhism directly challenged the hegemony of the soma priests as spiritual and ritual authorities, and whether soma was originally the fly agaric mushroom (Amanita muscaria), as Gordon Wasson believed, Syrian rue (Peganum harmala), as David Flattery suggested, or Psilocybe cubensis, ergotized barley or rye, marijuana (Cannabis sativa), or some other plant, its consciousness-altering powers are well documented. Its use was central to the Vedic religion that formed the cultural and religious milieu from which Buddhism sprang.

It also seems likely that the rejection of psychoactive plants was a rejection of shamanism, and because many or most of the plant doctors were probably women, thus a rejection of women as spiritual teachers. It is not clear which of the two concerns was most salient.

It is clear, though, that certain classes of psychoactive plants were once much more utilized by yogic practitioners, in India and throughout the world. More, it is clear that psychoactive plants (or animals!) have been a part of, or at the very center of, religious practice in the majority of prehistoric cultures, though I don't agree with those who say that psychoactive plants are the *only* possible origin of religion (death, to cite just one alternative, is another suitable candidate).

#############################

Traces remain, metaphors remain.

Early Buddhist psalms speak of *asava*, the "deadly drugs." The arhat is one who has freed himself from the four *asavas*: desire, speculation, ignorance, and rebirth (lust for life).

> *Asava:*
> *an extract or secretion of a tree or flower;*
> *an outflow, flowing, or emission;*
> *attention or desire, the soul,*
> *directed outwards toward an object—*
> *thus, infirmity, a drug, or poison.*

Images remain: Amitabha is called *amritaraja*, the Nectar-King.

> *Amrita. Ambrosia.*
> *The divine nectar. The Drink of Immortality.*

Amrita is closely connected to soma. The Tibetan translation for *amṛta* is *dutsi*. In the Buddhist version of the myth about churning the ocean to obtain ambrosia, Vajrapani turns black after drinking Rahu's *dutsi*-laden urine, as Shiva turns blue in the Hindu version.

In the dharani for feeding the hungry ghosts, we chant

> *Adoration to Kanroo the Tathagata.*

Kanroo: ambrosia. *Kan* plus *Lou*, bliss-bestowing nectar.

Buddha is the poison for poison. The Buddha-dharma is the Ambrosial Drum.

Nirvana is the *Nectar City*, the entrance is the Ambrosial Gate.

> *Amṛta:*
> *the deathless, the unborn.*
> *A sea of neurotransmitters. What is the solute?*

#################

But Buddhist yoga has not entirely abandoned chemical aids, in the quest for Realization. William McNeill, in *The Rise of the West*, states that Indian religiosity, and thence that of Christianity, Islam, and Chinese Buddhism, is founded and sustained by insights triggered by oxygen starvation.

A facile reduction, but perhaps with a pointer: shallow breathing, sometimes extremely shallow breathing, is indeed a salient feature of deep meditation. (Though it seems likely that the carbon dioxide level, more than that of the dissolved oxygen, would have the more profound pharmacological activity. Two of the therapeutic indications for carbon dioxide are "negativism" and "melancholia.")

Still, as Zen students know, the best technique is no guarantor of insight. You can enter a high, altered state of consciousness and go right on sleeping. Maybe the point is not to get high, but to come down.

> *But isn't that a high?*

################

> *Hui Neng was just chopping wood, nothing special.*
> *Always good to remember that.*

Still, it is the sesshin, the intense yogic training period, that is the context for most of our stories of *kensho*, Realization.

An altered state of consciousness.

Days of sitting. Pain in the legs. Not quite "sensory deprivation," but sustained, practiced focus and stillness. Bound to change one's neurochemistry: endorphins at least, and probably a lot more. And the change is often most apparent after leaving sesshin, re-entering the world and encountering familiar settings.

> *The "post-sesshin high."*

We can characterize it phenomenologically, as we can other drugs.

Effects: mental clarity; heightened empathic assessment of other people; strengthening of intuitive powers; possible diminishment of certain analytical syllogistic skills. High pain threshold.

Or, some parts like a mild opium high, perhaps combined with the alertness of cocaine (again, small dose); or like half a tab of MDMA without the jaw clenching. Or like a full tab of MDMA without the jaw clenching. And some playfulness, like, well,

> *A spring morning. Saturday morning.*
> *The birds! So many birds*
> *singing.*

Duration: Lasts for 12 to 48 hours after leaving sesshin. Gradual tapering of effects. Mild crash, completely mitigated by sleep and more meditation.

But as with any high, you have to come down. Aitken Roshi often makes this point during his post-sesshin cautions.

The students are warned that they are in a highly sensitized and energized state. They are warned about getting involved in philosophical and intellectual discussions, about driving (timing is often altered), that, though the mind is awake and alert, the body is nonetheless tired, perhaps exhausted, and will need rest. And, of course, to avoid dissipating the experience by talking about it too much.

It's not uncommon for sangha members who did not participate in the sesshin to show up for the closing ceremony and the informal meal, visiting, and cleanup that follows, just to feel the "energy" ("contact high," we used to call that).

# # # # # # # # # # # # # # # # #

> *"You have to come down."*

An altered state of consciousness acutely suited to one task, not necessarily optimal or even appropriate to others.

Are we agreed here? Are we all agreed on this point?

Altered state/nothing special.
Altered from what?
Altered implies a norm, an unaltered state of consciousness.

The matter of sobriety.

> *Hard to see, though, how an altered state of consciousness is necessary to perceive the truth of suffering.*

################

The term "drugs" won't do: which drugs? Neither will "sobriety." Sobriety from what? Alcohol sober, but high on cannabis? Or cannabis, alcohol, and caffeine sober but under the influence of cocaine?

Or maybe nicotine sober, Valium sober, and television sober, yet totally mad with love and jealousy.

Or drunk with rationality. Sober with attachment.

Drugs, as a general term, is an obfuscation of the War on Drugs. We hear the phrase "alcohol and drugs," as if alcohol were not a drug, and as if by drugs we all know what is being talked about. Addiction is an issue with tobacco, alcohol, and the opiates, but is not at all a property of the entheogens. Addiction to alcohol, a cellular poison, is characterized by physical and mental deterioration that is virtually absent in opiate addiction. Tobacco kills nearly half a million Americans each year, but there are no recorded deaths from marijuana. Each of these plants and substances has distinct properties, promises, and dangers. All that is served by lumping a group of them together is a government program of spiritual and political oppression aimed at cutting off all dialogue.

The War on Drugs is in essence a religious war. That is why drug offenders frequently get longer prison sentences than violent criminals. A drug user is worse than a criminal—no punishment is too severe, because drug users are heretics.

Our interest here is in a special class of psychoactive plants and drugs that have acquired spiritual reputations: *Psilocybe* mushrooms, peyote, ayahuasca, and LSD. They are even called *entheogens*, "manifesting-god-within," akin to the enthusiasm of the Greek desert fathers. Ecstasy.

#################

Meditation as a standard, a calibrating, measuring device. Meditation and koan practice as a control to assess different classes of psychotropic plants and substances.

Tea, Bodhidharma's gift, the Barbarian's own poison, his very eyelids given for the benefit of sentient beings in their quest for realization. Some argue that while tea is beneficial, coffee is disruptive. Some find that even tea is disturbing, strengthening the monkey more than the watcher.

Some say that MDMA is an excellent catalyst for the first day of sesshin.

> *Ahhh, what about guyusa leaves,*
> *so low in tannins, for a predawn tea?*
> *What about a good chew of khat,*
> *to subdue the drowsiness*
> *of a hot afternoon?*

The *Hevajra Tantra* mentions camphor as being drunk in certain rituals to gain *siddhi*. In small doses, camphor is a stimulant. but in large doses, administered intravenously, camphor was used to induce convulsions in mental patients, before it was replaced with electricity. Camphor is an isomer of thujone, the active oil in wormwood, *Artemisia absinthium*.

Trungpa singled out marijuana as being detrimental to meditation: saying that it mimicked meditation—and forbade its use and presence.

Almost everyone finds LSD much too powerful and overwhelming to be useful in practice.

Field Report, a poet and Rinzai practitioner.

I took some LSD during a sesshin while I was in Japan. It was too much, too exaggerated. Everything was too perfect and meaningful. The timing and sound of the bells had cosmic significance. The monks were so beautiful that I wanted to cry. Everything was so numinous.

[Did you get a koan answer?]

Oh yes. I found a great, perfect answer.

[Did you go to dokusan?]

Yes.

[And . . . ?]

Oh, it was wrong, of course. I mean I had a great, perfect answer, but it wasn't the point of the koan at all.

# # # # # # # # # # # # # # # #

The salient feature of entheogens in American Buddhism at present is memorial: that many Americans were attracted to Buddhism in the first place because of psychedelic revelations. If, as some pedants claim, such experiences are not "genuine," their persistence is remarkable indeed.

Very few dedicated students seem interested in using psychedelics WITHIN the context of the Buddha-way, but even fewer recant the importance or significance of their previous experiences. Most of them claim that the Buddha-way is a natural extension or progression of their psychedelic experiences. Many leave open the possibility of renewing their acquaintance with entheogenic plants or substances in the future.

Maybe it's not that visionary plants and drugs are useful for Zen training, but that Zen training is excellent preparation for using psychedelic drugs.

No amount of meditation is going to give you an LSD experience.

#################

Is there something MISSING, a barren area in Buddhism, that these sacred plants and medicines address?

We had all walked down to the beach. It seems like everyone was talking at once. Tim was crying and laughing at the same time, came over and started hugging me.

"All this time, my whole life, I've been embarrassed about my teeth—that's all it was—so I wouldn't smile—just because of my teeth I've been stopping myself from smiling."

This promise, this chance, that through insight, revelation, through discovered/recovered facility, that obstacles be dissolved and the ego be strengthened and healed.

Crying and laughing, hugging.

At any point on this continuum, the matter of the fifth precept may be addressed.

#################

Surāmeraya-majjappa-mādahānā
veramanīṣikkhāpadaṁsamādiyāmi

"I undertake the training rule to abstain from fermented and distilled intoxicants which are the basis for heedlessness."

Surā refers to spiritous, flavored liquors, though it is not clear that this has always specifically meant distilled alcoholic beverages, as five kinds of surā are mentioned in the *Veda. Meraya* refers to any sort of fermented beverage: Rhys Davids says that there were five kinds. *Majja* is an intoxicant, from a very ancient Indo-European root with cognates that include words for mead, madness, passion, and rejoicing. Rhys Davids suggests "indolence" for *pamada* instead of "heedlessness."

The most literal interpretation of the precept is clearly directed against alcohol, and, more specifically, against its deleterious effects on mindfulness and morality. Opium, at the time of the *Vinaya* was almost certainly viewed purely as a medicine and not as an intoxicant. The absence of *bhang* from the precept, however, may be significant, because hemp was indeed used in some yogic practices, and has left traces in both Hindu and Buddhist tantra.

Bhikkhu Bodhi stresses the heedlessness that arises from intoxication as the point of the precept.

> *Under the influence of intoxicants a man who might otherwise be restrained can lose self-control, become heedless, and engage in killing, stealing, adultery, and lying. Abstinence from intoxicants is prescribed on the grounds that it is essential to the self-protection of the individual and for the well-being of family and society. The precept thus prevents the misfortunes that result from the use of intoxicants: loss of wealth, quarrels and crimes, bodily disease, loss of reputation, shameless conduct, negligence, and madness.*
>
> —Bhikkhu Bodhi, *Going For Refuge*

But we have to go further. We will not dally in the literal. The precept is about delusions.

> *But sobriety also deludes.*
> *If sobriety did not delude,*
> *there would be no Buddhists,*
> *no one lighting incense and chanting Kanzeon.*

The precept is about not muddying the waters.

But there is something muddy about many commentaries on the fifth precept, when "intoxicants" are glossed in a lump to "drugs." Characterizations such as "semiconscious euphoria," or "heedless loss of self-control," or "haze that clouds the mind" bear little affinity with the ecstatic epiphanies and insights of the psychedelic experience.

Still. Such ignorance should not limit our own investigations. We know something about delusion, and something about the seductive powers of Mara's beautiful daughters.

> *Self-nature is subtle and mysterious. In the realm of the intrinsically pure Dharma, not giving rise to delusion is called the Precept of Not Giving or Taking Drugs.*
>
> —Bodhidharma

################

Dogen is more karmic:

> *Drugs have not been brought into it. Don't bring them in.*

Which drugs? Bodhidharma's eyelids? Carbon dioxide volume?

In another sense the poisons were there from the beginning. Maybe they *are* the beginning: a grand hallucination of seeming. Of eyes, taste, touch, thought, and object of thought.

> *Birth, death, and dreaming:*
> *beta-carbolines shielding tryptamines,*
> *carbohydrates in a controlled burn.*
> *Rice as a powerful hallucinogen.*

################

Medicinal use of drugs is excepted from the precept.

We bless the rice and vegetables we eat at sesshin as "this good medicine."

And supper is considered "medicine," not a meal at all—therefore not transgressing the rule that monks eat only twice a day.

> *Yun Men, teaching his community, said, "Medicine and disease subdue each other: the whole earth is medicine; what is your self?"*
> *—Blue Cliff Record, case 87*

The earth comes forth to confirm the self: tonight's cold wind; a warm cup of soup.

Different diseases require different medicines.

> *But are we not ill? Dukkha?*
> *Are we not, like all conditioned and composite dharmas, ill?*
> *And is not one of the greatest illnesses the frozen, reified*
> *belief in the ultimate nature of external objects?*
> *Or its converse?*

# # # # # # # # # # # # # # # # #

The question of entheogenic drugs more generally is the question of ecstatic visions. Divine madness. *Makyō.*

Makyō: the Path of Illusions; Path of Dreams. A feeling of great numinosity.

Makyō.

魔境

Ma, hemp-spirit, Mara, the devil in the phenomenal world. Makyō are visions that appear at certain stages of the meditation path.

> *A deep dream of participation in the Buddha Dharma.*
> —Robert Aitken

The *Surangama Sutra* lists fifty types of makyō, ten for each of the five aggregates of form, receptiveness, conceptions, discrimination, and consciousness. The Buddha states that these visions are harmless, even excellent progressive stages, unless the practitioner believes that they signify complete attainment.

> *In the clear and penetrating state of your mind when it looks within, its light appears in all its purity and at midnight you will suddenly see in your dark room all sorts of apparitions as clearly as in broad daylight, with all the other objects usually there. This is the mind, in its subtlety, refining its clear perceptions which enables you to see distinctly in the dark. This temporary achievement does not mean you are a saint. If you do not regard it as such, it is an excellent progressive stage, but if you do you will give way to demons.*
>
> —*Surangama Sutra*

# # # # # # # # # # # # # # # # #

To poison poison, the Peacock Path. The way of transmutation.

The blue color of the peacock is the blue of Shiva, the blackness of Vajrapani: the color of the poison-drinker.

> *In the jungles of poisonous plants strut the peacocks…*

The Bodhisattva of Makyō, the Poison Buddha, The Bodhisattva of Illusions: the buddha with 108,000 names who teaches and saves with illusion. Whose very name poisons preconceptions, who leaves us in a soup of dreams.

We know this path in our imaginations, or is it our memories? A path that includes ecstasy and ecstatic visions, the God of Ecstasy, Shiva, or maybe Dionysus: the Bodhisattva who gave us his very blood as a medicine for crippling inhibitions, that the true soul emerge.

Dionysus, by nature unrecognized, but surely present in the pantheon: a young god with the rank of bodhisattva.

Iconography: sometimes rides a panther, sometimes an ass. Androgynous. Usually with long hair. Associated with the thyrsus and tambourine, wears a garland of ivy leaves (a cure for drunkenness). God of music, poetry, song, and the theater. Dharani may include eating wild mushrooms and raw flesh (emblematic of the food web and interdependence).

Associated with springtime, and an ecstatic state of consciousness often mistaken for madness, but more appropriately named Great Joy. Enthusiastic exuberance.

Wrathful aspect: hawk eating a ground squirrel; cat playing with a mouse, waiting, letting it revive and run in order to catch it again. Two schoolgirls catching fireflies, pulling the abdomens off and sticking them onto their arms and the back of their hands, dancing and laughing, their jewelry aglow with green light.

Let a thousand schools flourish, the way of Buddhism is assimilation, not rejection. The Divine Madness school of Buddhism, watched over by the Bodhisattva Dionysus, who uses enthusiasm and ecstatic visions as devices...

> *And thus Bodhisattvas are likened to peacocks:*
> *They live on delusions—those poisonous plants.*
> *Transforming them into the essence of Practice,*
> *They thrive in the jungle of everyday life.*
> *Whatever is presented they always accept,*
> *While destroying the poison of clinging desire.*
> —Dharmarakshita

#################

iconography sometimes rides a panther, sometimes an ass. Androgynous. Usually with long hair. Associated with the thyrsus and tambourine, [illegible] a garland of ivy leaves (a cure for drunkenness). God of music, poetry, [illegible], and the theater. [illegible] may include [illegible] with [illegible] and raw flesh [illegible] of the food [illegible].

Associated with [illegible] and ecstatic states [illegible] madness, [illegible] by [illegible] ecstasy.

[illegible]

[illegible]

[illegible]

[illegible]
[illegible]
[illegible] into the essence of reality,
[illegible] in the jungle of [illegible]
[illegible]
[illegible]
—[illegible]

PAT REED was born in 1956 under the landing patterns of LAX (Los Angeles International Airport), and grew up with her feet in the Pacific Ocean. She practiced violin concertos in her walk-in closet until her discovery of poetry at age nineteen, when she moved to the San Francisco Bay Area which was the center of a decades-long West Coast poetry revival. There she has written poetry, surfed, studied literature at the University of California, Berkeley, and practiced in the Soto lineage of Zen with Reb Anderson at Green Gulch Farms Zen Center and Mel Weitsman at the Berkeley Zen Center. She has taught South East Asian immigrants for over a decade and is currently working on a non-fiction book about Vietnamese refugees in Oakland. Pat marches with Fiddlers for Peace and performs on the fiddle in the Bay Area's energetic folk music subculture. Her work has been published primarily by small literary presses dedicated to innovative writings—some in hand-set letterpress format, some in samizdat photocopy format, others as conventional books. These include *Sea Asleep* (Coincidence Press), *More Awesome* and *Qualm Lore* (One Dog Garage), *Nagrivator* (Xena Bird), *Kismet* (from Leslie Scalapino's O Books), *We Want To See Your Tears Falling Down* (Literatura de Cordel), *Container of Stars* (Acturus Editions), and *Lost Coast* (Other Publications). Her recent work has appeared in *Nocturnes*, *Crayon*, and *Enough*. She lives in Oakland, California.

CONTAINER OF STARS

FIRE

poking
through the
black grid

river pouring
off in the
starlight

which is
whiter

I didn't sit
by the
soft lake

I climbed some
more to the
hard mirror-
bright one

tried to sleep
on the slanted
granite

turned away
from the white
sun

one bird making
a ruckus

cliffs sealing up
its sound

. ˙ .

Aspen
flip't the sun-
light

and the speckled deer
bound at me

blink't big eye
lifted an ear

swiveled its head
& tore at the
thorny berry

. ˙ .

A cup,
a CONTAINER
of stars

and the stream
falls off the mountain

torn white

goes green
in a deepness

ribbons over
clear-spun
crash

puzzles through
the crush of logs

divining
down

.˙.

The mountains
up there
in the dark

why want to be
up on their cold
slopes

exposed

while the stars
stick in the trees
down here

and the fire
works the side
of the log

.˙.

Someone who'd
been with me

got up with me
and walked in my body

over to get some

more
wood

for the fire

at my feet

under triangled stars

.˙.

I climbed
anyway
into cold
green

which barely
parted
for me as if

too cold to
ripple

I walked inside
the water

then walked back
to the pale
sun

floundering outside
a part of the wind

.˙.

The night has
got a grip
on the tops
of the pines

and all the way
to the bottom
solid

dark hours before
I can sleep
I sit in the woods

burning things

all the water
boiled away

5 days of
dirty hands

and trying to find
the toothbrush
in the dark

.˙.

The dark
star
I mean
the dark
around the star

gone deep

from far away
comes a rattle

up the rough road
bangs a rickety cage

to take the horses
home for the winter

VERY STILL

then the water
closed me
cold

& wind came
from winter

fish whump
and her bracelet
rang

pushed off
and found deeper rock

the grass
lying down
on the water

melted
lake in a granite
fracture

naked
and made to swim

birds on the
reaches
& roar of some wind

.˙.

My mind has a heat
with the sun slung low
and sliding

equinox quick
bugs rising
a minute of their song

one bird
says more

and the lake comes to me
with its woven
mountains

the poem
wants to weep

the summer done

the green didn't
notice my
swim

STREAM

gone bright
the aspen quivered

coal-black
leaves

in these
aloneness grows

pine lean
broken at the top

climbing &
frayed struck
& tangled against
moon-cloud

nothing to warm or cool
the moon

it burns & freezes

stretches up
one face
opens the blackness

.˙.

Giants shift
in a pre-storm wind

shin-high fire
melts my shoe

pants at the bark
dragged from the wet
meadow

∴

Under black
pagodas

I sit still
in my tent
by the river

filling my ear
with cold going

what pulls it down
through the rocks

makes a pool
torn green
heart

spilling in the granite

I want to get
to the other side

to a mound of sun
but fear the falling

∴

Wade again
through dark hours

'til the moon
lays daggers
at the feet of the trees

face hot
from the fire
staring into the dark
bears somewhere sleeping

good
to sleep
for a season

& wake
forgetful
in a wet spring

∴

Stubborn fire
collapsing

dowsing me
in smoke

my eyes sting
I jump

& turn to the
dark river

∴

Aspen shake
soundless

and rain falls
in the sun

tiny honeymoon cottage
perched on the river
locked up tight

a young buck
hooves steep rock

drifts his wary head at me

bounds the spring
and springs the mountain

up to a grey brother

∴

Up the red-rocked
falls
far up
the catchings
and pour-
ings
slippery rock
and caught log

one bird sang
while it flew
blue
to blue juniper

no one to
catch
still wanting
to climb

pulled up
pool to pool
by bits of its
call

.˙.

Down in the valley
after the rain
white horses
roll in the dust

. ˙ .

Moon-
rise

the pines
rinse out
their darkness

and cottonwood
whiten

the roar of my fire
bodes a quick end

and stars slide under
night-white clouds

the earth-wheel
turns

and river goes down

burning bark
goes belly-up

and the underside glows
unreadable
red fortune

caves and faces

that slowly go dark
but warm
awhile

—Last camper in the campground,
Mineral King,
Fall equinox

JANET RODNEY

CONCEIVED, her mother told her, "on a Dutch ship traveling the Indian Ocean from China to Capetown," born in 1941 in Washington D.C., Janet Rodney spent her early years in Washington and New York. Her father was killed in the Salomon Islands in 1942. After living with her mother in France and Switzerland, and for a year in Taiwan where she acquired an elementary knowledge of Chinese and studied Chinese brush, she moved to Spain, remaining until age 33. From 1964–66 Rodney was married to Gabriel Ferrater, a Catalan poet. She has published translations from both Spanish and Persian in various anthologies, including Milkweed Edition's *Mouth to Mouth: Poems by Twelve Contemporary Mexican Women*. She is a digital artist, poet, and letterpress printer. In 1987 she founded Weaslesleeves Press Inc., and produces fine letterpress books that are now in museum and library collections across the country. She began to receive Zen teachings in 1981, spent four years with the Zen Studies Society in New York City, and was eventually ordained a lay nun *(upasika)* by Eido Roshi in 1985, shortly before she moved to New Mexico. In 1996 she began Tibetan Buddhist studies with Lobsang Lhalungpa. She currently lives outside Santa Fe with her husband, Nathaniel Tarn. Her books of poetry include *Chameleon's Cadmium*, *Orphydice*, the collaborative volume *Alashka* written with Tarn, and *The Book of Craving*, a fine letterpress edition with photomontage by the author, printed at Grey Spider Press in 1997.

BARDO OF LEAVING

FOR ED DORN

You are now traversing
I know not what ocean
or spaceroom of atoms,
vessel of light
and tensile strength,
heading out from what was
a uniquely versatile craft
on the swell of the 20th century.

Nothing now in the way of mindforms
will now allow a change of course:
not a situation that would
normally spring to mind,
in connection with your person.

You stand under a cottonwood tree,
portrait larger than life.
Wind blows and
your face breaks up in leaves,
wind stops, your face comes back,
thus three times or so.

Later you say,
Got the message?
Face or leaves it's all one.

Keep looking.

BARDO OF PERCEPTION

FOR TED ENSLIN

Imagine this scene in a desolate place
on the banks of the Nairanjana,

it is lying very still,
the mind's coiled rope,
at dusk, the direction
you walk in doesn't feel
like mere thought,

a snake appearing in the way
is not earth or water,
nor are you or it
fire or space, nor are you
or the snake its or your awareness
or air, or all your parts together,

or anything other
than all of these.

BARDO OF WRITING

It can be said poets
talked too much
wrote too long,
listening to the sound
of their voices.

This was my offering
to have written little,
&
heard the sounds
of the world.

MIRIAM SAGAN

MIRIAM SAGAN was born April 27, 1954 in Manhattan, then raised in New Jersey. She received a B.A. from Harvard and an M.A. in creative writing from Boston University. In the early 1980s she and her husband, Robert Winson, studied at San Francisco Zen Center. They moved to New Mexico with Richard Baker Roshi in the early eighties—she describes it as Robert following his teacher and she following her husband—and co-authored *Dirty Laundry: 100 Days in a Zen Monastery* during a residency at Baker Roshi's Crestone, Colorado, center. In Santa Fe Miriam followed Philip Whalen around (who had also moved there as a student of Baker Roshi), taking care of the older poet, learning what she could through their companionship about the art of poetry, and eating hamburgers with him. One of New Mexico's more visible poets, teachers, and literary activists, she is the author of a dozen books of poetry, non-fiction, and fiction. After the death of her husband Robert, who had been ordained a priest in the Soto lineage of Zen, she wrote *Searching for Mustard Seeds*, an account of her coming to terms with his death and what spiritual practice could mean in her new life. Her titles of poetry include the acclaimed *The Art of Love*, which gathered new and selected poems in 1994, and most recently *Rag Trade*, both titles from La Alameda Press of Albuquerque. She is poetry columnist for *Writer's Digest* and edits the e-zine *Santa Fe Poetry Broadside*.

CONTENTMENT

Woke up to the finches crowing
Peeked into a nest, male and female sitting together
Looking out with sleepy beady finch eyes
Not like waking up 2 AM
Thinking of Frank dying in New York City
And angry at everyone because dying is so expensive
Last night driving up Cerro Gordo road
I remembered how I'd forgotten New Mexico again and again
And the foothills lay like little girls on their sides
Covered in scrub and snow.
Stars out and all the unidentified shining objects:
Planets, planes, space shuttle debris
Halley's comet, handmirror, handmaiden,
A pool of water—star bathing
Star as a woman—healing water—
Ojo Caliente—she keeps glowing—
Long haired angel of midnight not of morning—
Easy—this girl for wooing—
Song—spiral—downward—maze for threading—
Labyrinth—the body's cunt and asshole—
Knife in hand and star arising
Over island, desert, fall-out
Watershed, in helium brewing
All things simultaneous
Over the little park
Over the road of dirt
Over the rim of the world
Over the blue of the wide
Over the before and after
Over the call and laughter

The universe, contented in its curve.
Philip, fat Zen priest, bald head, old, perfect, cranky
Playing baroque music on the Casio keyboard
And the cat Lily illegally and happily curled on his blanket
Room like a curio shop in San Francisco Chinatown
Long crystals, fossils, Buddhas, odd blue deities
And a white ceramic Bodhisattva
With an unconvincing number of arms
And Philip told me "you can ring the bells"
And I rang this long strand of metal cowbells from Tibet
That sounded like Pema the thanka painter's hand clasp
Felt warm and green/brown in high up country.
Once Pema showed me a picture
"This is my uncle's horse," he said
In a tone of such happiness
At being related to everybody.
Philip's room fills me with greed
And a sense that we are going to die
Greed because he will probably die before I do
And then I will get the chance to have something of his.
What I meant to say . . .
What I meant to say is . . .
What I meant . . .
That time my favorite finch died
I ran into the kitchen crying and said to Philip and my husband
Promise you won't die, ever!
And Philip said: I'm afraid you got to us a little too late for that.

YOJIMBO

Outside the house: lilacs, white and lilac
Inside the house: filmstrip of a wandering samurai
Listen to me. I get paid for killing.
Outside the house: crickets and more crickets
Inside the house: crickets.
Slant on a roof. Light between the wooden slats.
The grey cat. A woman in a white under robe.
Listen to me. I get paid for killing.
Black and white leaves in a black and white wind.

He said he had a dream: that long ago
He and my husband were priests on horses.
Outside the house: a shadow, Yojimbo
Listen to me. I get paid for killing.
A sliding screen. Inside the house:
A scroll painting—
Red demon,
Woman giving birth on her side
And Shakyamuni Buddha
Pointing at the moon.

Outside the house, my house: the irrigation ditch,
  dandelions shut in darkness
Blue mountains I can't stop talking about
And the dream's wildness of red haired Jews
With their violins and suitcases,
Wandering.
Outside my house: lilacs
Inside my house: a plate of green black eggplant
Maybe you're wondering why I'm telling you this

Listen to me. I get paid for killing.
Unable, finally to empty my thought,
Empty: this mind: not: empty.

MOUNTAIN PEAK GRAVE

Plant a corkscrew willow
On your grave—
I'd rather leave my bra
After all, you loved women
Even more than trees.

I'm just a laywoman
We don't mean the same thing
The calligraphy in translation reads
Existence and non-existence
Are the same.

Monks of this mountain monastery
You eat cold soup
From a cold bowl
When will you depart
And start following the way?

PRAYER FLAG

Wood is not the past tense of fire,
The future of fire is not ash,
Someone or other gave us this green prayer flag
And we forgot all about it in the hall closet.
Luck is not the past tense of water wheel
Although Genghis Khan may be the future tense of city,
Nomad is the past tense of Jew,
A word with the future tense of messiah.
The pottery army stands firm in the ground
Guarding the tomb of the long dead king
Six thousand life size figures
Stare forward into nothing.
The archeologist is still just a girl
With her hair caught in a pink chiffon scarf
Her hands hold a brush, minister delicately
To the mute remnant of impossible desire.
At the great tomb on the Silk Road
Who cut off the hands and heads
Of every figure of an ambassador
Carved along the avenue?
The past tense of Marco Polo is Italy,
My present tense is full of potted geraniums
The prayer flag hangs from the portal
Over the woodpile and the Mexican sunflowers.
Wind that doesn't stop day or night
Raises the green lotus in the air.
The future tense of oasis is sand,
Even pottery tokens stamped with the Buddha
Lie exposed like pebbles on the tide of the desert.
This prayer flag comes from Lama mountain
Actually, there is no wind at all
The air is still, it is the flag that is moving.

The past tense of fire is fire
The future tense of ash is ash
A pink rosebush climbs the front wall of our house—
Look, it's just about to bloom.

READING CHIYO-NI, 1703–1775, JAPANESE WOMAN HAIKUIST

all night I quarrel with you in my dreams
the child who wants to return to the sea
the mother who wants to keep her
in Edo Japan, widows, whores and nuns write haiku
a path through oak trees, or the way of the tao
day three on the tramp steamer she ran out of things to read
we went to see the volcano's steam vents despite the rain
holding up one black umbrella
a butter-colored cat I had never seen before stalking the perimeter of the field
snail shell broken on the sidewalk
my daughter woke and interrupted my handwriting
statue of the famous woman poet stands facing the New England harbor
each button cast in bronze
a notion of impermanence, an actual alteration of the shoreline
monuments to the dead whose names meant nothing to us
in the town square, or on marble tombstones obscured by moss
you could count seventeen syllables your whole life
you could try to follow the mind
you could see instead
a falling down barn and house
field of Queen Anne's lace
goldenrod
orange butterfly
you could . . .

SOUTH RIDGE ZENDO

Walking to Philip's downhill in the rain
A bird embryo on the sidewalk
Zazen organizes events around itself
Like opening or closing a green umbrella.

Tears begin when I sit with incense
Like the smell of you late last night
Hair full of smoke and earth
As you pull my pants off in bed.

Bowing together now
An unopened rosebud on the altar.
Outside in raindrops we can't stop laughing:
Did you see Philip pull that thread out of his robe?

Mindless, happy, going home I am singing
All Buddhas, ten directions, three times
I've Got A Right To Sing The Blues and
Buddy Can You Spare A Dime.

Climbing uphill, an almost full moon
Hits me like a moan in the belly
And I turn to look and *see*
White bell flowers heavy on the stem.

LESLIE SCALAPINO

BORN IN 1947, Leslie Scalapino attended Reed College, then earned an M.A. in English from the University of California, Berkeley. She has been a prolific poet, novelist, playwright, and essayist, pioneering mixed forms such that she can speak of essays that are plays and novels that are poems. Active in the San Francisco Bay Area's lively poetry scenes of the 1970s and '80s, and occasionally identified with the avant-garde experiments of language poetry, she has also been an active member of Poets Theater, and has collaborated with poets, playwrights, and visual artists. She founded and continues to publish O Books, whose authors range from active elders like Michael McClure to young, just-emerging writers, whose work she has loyally championed at a time when more visible presses prefer to publish established names. Anthologies Scalapino has published include work that has protested both Gulf wars, the most recent being *War and Peace.* She is a frequent traveler in Asia and has written of the influence of poetic diaries by women of Japan's Heian period on her own writing, as well as the impact of photography and film. Her many books include *Zither & Autobiography.* In *Autobiography* Scalapino studies the shifts and repetitions of memory: "fixed memories move as illusions." Her book *The Public World / Syntactically* explores similarities between Zen thought and American experimental writing. Recent poetry titles include *New Time* and *The Front Matter, Dead Souls* from Wesleyan University Press and a small volume from Post-Apollo Press, from which the pages in this collection are excerpted.

from IT'S GO IN/ QUIET ILLUMINED GRASS/ LAND

silver half freezing in day
elation the
outside
of the outside sky walking
rose

silver half freezing in day
moon's elation
of the outside rose, his seeing
on both
'sides'
seeing someone else at all and the
half freezing
elation of the outside so that's even
with one
continually over and over one/person

he will
also now person dying? is not
compared to
space they're in outside silver freezing
half
moon day now both walking rose
instant
running — wall — wall

comparing the mind to magnolias
or to sky, because one sees.
but comparing people's actions to sky
or to war to moon outside? is in that space
then.
apprehend
behavior-evening — ferocity even
from just one — where there was no reason
bewildering — doesn't seem
'bewildering' if it's huge in multitude.
indentation so that they're even
one to evening — is no behavior-evening
any event a random space

wall standing rose could just
'place'
together
as evening in the middle of
people
speaking
and so no space even there
one?
freezing pale night at wild (only)
day
'there' only, no rose even so can
'place'
the day there being no people

speaking
one

Always stay in
the quiet illumined grass
land — but I can't — do it
there being other people there
to
just do
it only staying in the grass land
illumined
'place' it together is 'land' and
comes out
just
do it

He just stays in
illumined grass land
has
just stayed always in it
in
events going on there and
the
outside
of illumined grass land comes
out

separate
standing wall of freezing evening
ones
are

if the mind's repetition at stages one's
only O rungs sun rose outside of
one's
junk place waking evening land
have
that
just — do it — land stay in
comes out

examin
ing
dreamed looking down
in
bush that's huge forest leaveless
fan
my needing place to live in dream,
the
next day
see forest leaveless fans hill up
vertically
light leaveless array fan
is this the same as

— is leaves, both — seeing —

examin
ing
the forest rose wall as
white in outside

and
dark green early forest not different
from rose
after (it) rose leaveless fan-
dawn
one?

hell
-pressure
skin
or passages in time
in
excruciating pain physically so the
time
passages
are gone. lifted, it's go
so there's
now
no time here it is spring bare
limbs
blossom blossoms 'on' bare limbs
'have'
the blossoms?

seen
leaveless forest in dream by
looking downwards
so (?) looking up the next day see
leaveless
fan-forest above
there
are no 'passages' outside

either
in time going or one
outside rose
'after one'

Can't be
in 'night'
as outside it is just 'day one's in'

either time or duration

excruciating physical pain hell
night *not*

is there.
'night night'

ANDREW SCHELLING

BORN IN 1953, Andrew Schelling grew up in "Thoreau territory," the townships west of Boston. Early attractions were to New England's wilder landscapes, as well as Asian art collections in the region. In 1973 he traveled to India and the Nepalese Himalayas for the first time, then settled in Northern California. He received a B.A. from U.C. Santa Cruz followed by Sanskrit studies at Berkeley. During the 1980s he lived in the Bay Area, where he co-edited the samizdat poetics journal *Jimmy & Lucy's House of "K,"* and made regular excursions into Sierra Nevada and Coast Range mountains. He first practiced zazen with Kobun Chino (Otokawa) Roshi in Santa Cruz, then studied at the Berkeley Zen Center. In 1990 Schelling moved to Colorado. Principal interests are in anthropology, natural history, and Asian literatures, and he remains an ardent mountain explorer. His books of poetry include *The Road to Ocosingo*, a Basho-inspired haibun (mixed prose & verse) account of a trip to Chiapas, Mexico, after the Zapatista revolution; *Two Elk Notebook*; and *Tea Shack Interior: New & Selected Poetry*. His recent *Wild Form, Savage Grammar: Poetry, Ecology, Asia* gathers ten years of essays. He has published five books of translation from ancient India's poetry, including works of Mirabai, early Buddhist wanderers, and classical Sanskrit poets. Most recent is *Erotic Love Poems from India* (Shambhala, 2004). He sits zazen at Hokubai Temple's buddha-yurt, studies at the feet of the Indian Peaks Wilderness, and teaches poetry and Sanskrit at Naropa University.

HAIBUN

Rock is naturalist scripture. The deeper you go the older the story.
Pikas & squirrels scamper over the top, then spiral descent
from gone tooth & twig. Petrified bone sediment myth.
Or psychic fossil? Horsetail & algae glow green again,
come to life in car engines. Fantastic shapes, old as forests.
And now the likelihood we have in the world
as many diverse minds. . . "as there are
organisms capable of perception."

Evolution's basic
job—turning rock
to green growth.

HAIBUN FLYCATCHER

How interesting that in 12th century Japan Saigyo remark'd, "I know nothing about depths in the composition of poetry." So dewdrop reflection of moon & wasted cherryblossom quavering branch are the trace of a buddha passing through our world?

What about piñon & various flycatcher species?

Today it is cottonwood boughs that seem wasted, withered in the great mandala of drought. At the studio door a flycatcher leaps. Has she stopped over briefly, on her seasonal trip? Dear Marlow, songbirds migrate at night, while we are dreaming. How precious to meet you this lifetime. You & this feathered eco-deity. The odds are improbable. The field guide says flycatchers are tough to distinguish. Encounter a nest, listen in on a love song, then let it go south with no name.

Migration pilgrim road—
what sort of creature
gets to the end of it?

A temple administrator spoke through the dream. *Though all things in this world undergo change, the way of poetry extends unaltered to the very last age.* The Willow flycatcher's poem sounds like a "sneezy fitz-bew," but I'm starting to think her a Cordillera: that "thin, squeaky pseet-trip-seet." For sure she's a comrade to fly with.

Bright eye-ring glint
pale wing bar glance
juniper pure land quiver.

27:xi:02

TYGER TYGER

The small outfit of contemporary techno-wizards who've taken up digs at The House of William Blake had some Americans by for a visit in May. Seventeen South Molton Street—last standing residence where William and Catherine Blake lived. The neighborhood's pricey these days, the global economy whirrs past its door, and sharply outfitted women go hunting for clothes. *Milton* and *Jerusalem* got written in second floor rooms, a sizable hand press stood by the window that fronts the street.

The good people in residence at the Blake house have almost no relics, but they did bring out a single archival box—stencils for *Milton*—also showed us wide modern drafting tables and high-end computer monitors used like bellows and anvil for angelic techno-designs out of Hell. Biscuits sat by the firebox where Blake once burnt coal. There was wine and a white British cheese. Warmed by the hospitality of our gentle hosts, and considering that the tiger Blake observed at the London Zoo had been brought out of India, I reframed a stanza of *Tyger* to Sanskrit. Had nobody tried it before? Surely some ganja-headed pundit of old Bengali renaissance days—?

śārdūla śārdūla ratrivaneṣu
tejaḥ prajvalan
ko 'ṃrtaḥ hasto vā chaksur vā
te bhīmaṃ rūpaṃ kartuṃ śaknoti

*

Early June, home to the Colorado foothills, west by a tiger's hair of the 105th Meridian. Icy mist holds the Front Range. It crawls down from the summits through boulder-choked canyons, leaving needles of frost on dark Douglas fir. Evening it vanishes upwards. Red Dakota hogbacks slip forth, a glimpse of smoky forest ravines that drop from Indian Peaks. Then precipice moon.

Who wandered these forests when Blake was setting *Tyger* to verse?
Ute Indians mostly. A few tough Frenchmen out trapping beaver.
And *did he smile his work to see?*

The region's dominant cat is *Felis concolor*—cougar, catamount, puma—mountain lion or painter—depends where in N. American space you picked up your speech. A Tupi Indian word passed to French trappers. Or archaic Greek, bent to the way things get said Upper South.

painter : panther : *Panthera tigris*

Caught in a coyote snare
on the Uncompahgre plateau,
I saw you there
thy tawny pelt
thy pelt philosophic & tattered
thy stiff drying deer-color'd pelt—

Blake died in 'twenty-five. Five years earlier Dr. Edwin James went up Blue Cloud Summit, botanizing the tundra, and named the mountain for Zebulon Pike. In '06 Pike had gone through and put cat tracks into his army report. By which time William Blake had turned upside-down a full notebook, and was drafting *Tyger* and *London* on the same empty page. The Southern Rockies were still Louisiana—blank on maps in the London cartographer shops.

Hail catamount,
tawny end-of-tail flicker once glimpsed as the
mesa grass stirr'd,
or felt dread feet when the stars
threw down their spears over high twilit
meadow alone—?

A scrape of dirt & debris, whiff of sharp urine
muddy track in the gloam.
Lay it down Tyger Tyger for humans—
& frame old symmetries
new poems.

10: vi: 98

A PERFECTION OF WISDOM SUITE

The *Prajna-paramita* or Perfection of Wisdom is a collection of Buddhist texts that appeared in India and central Asia 2000 years ago. The term Perfection of Wisdom refers also to the teachings contained in these texts, laid out most succinctly in the *Diamond* and *Heart* sutras. In India and along the Silk road, the Prajna-paramita was venerated as a great wisdom goddess; some of the longer sutras tenderly pronounce her Mother of Buddhas, and intriguingly, "womb of the bodhisattva." Her teachings were delivered by Buddha to his most advanced students, then due to their confounding paradoxes entrusted to the nagas (guardian serpent dragons) for preservation under deep roiling river waters. In the 2nd or 3rd century, Nagarjuna retrieved them & put them to work as the basis for his mind-cracking metaphysics.

Traveling to London in December 2002, I hoped to handle Sanskrit poetry manuscripts & some original Buddhist material in the British Library's India & Oriental Offices before heading by train into Wales. In that huge modern brick vault next to St. Pancras—it holds the loot of centuries—an 11th or 12th century "Prajna-paramita in 8000 Lines" from Nepal seemed to stir within its wrap of crisp yellow linen....

HYMNS FOR THE PERFECTION OF WISDOM IN PARADISE

A BOOK FOR MARLOW

I had fallen asleep, my hand on your belly. Rain fell across the wooded flanks of the Blorenge. Fog concealed the village of Llanellen below. In the dream I was studying the soft textured flesh of your torso. Two scripts appeared, English and Sanskrit, tattooed across your belly. I tried but could read neither. A slight echo, as of speech, from your womb.

*

Snake-like
an intelligence struggles upwards
centuries old moisture had
moldered some
fibers
the warped paper, flecks of silvering ink
gone into solution
O brick-like collection of verse
once known as
womb of all Buddhas

*

In the earlier poem I had asked what

do we do if the nagas
awaken
where could we go?
how could we stand?
That the text's
guardians would follow us
through the island
— four billion year rock—
who might have guessed?

Ragged half
inch by half inch
thundercloud-paper,
color of Krishna. The tiniest relic—

*

Sexual passion is the irreducible
element
this phrase came into
the notebook,
another book counseled—
dragons in the countryside struggling
their blood yellow & indigo

Then a gold-leaf diagram: constellations the
cold
interstellar heavens
twisting

*

Jean Arp discovered chance composition
when he tore up a failed drawing. Scattering

the shreds he noticed the
curious beauty
a new
configuration on the floor.

*

Gambhira : depth :
water is the domain of
the nagas they
coil through the texts & into

Mother of Buddhas

regarding the world as a dream

nirukti-prati-samvid
knowledge-of-languages
taraka timiram dipo mayavashyaya budbudam
all compounded things regarded as
dewdrop, as bubble.
"I could…

murder a cup of tea—"
Cherry, gnarled oak, moss-entrenched beech & holly
the holly alight with red berries
berries alight in the
impenetrable fog
the forests of Wales

Gwylfa'r Mynydd
Mountain Lookout
21:xii:02

*

From the Sugarloaf
due south of the Brecon Beacons
these we recorded—

hooker's green
raw sienna
burnt umber
pale Naples yellow
russet
windsor

caramel bunchgrass
dusty blue sage
dusty rose
rose madder
lichen
chartreuse
hunter's green

The Perfection of Wisdom reveals
herself
among mountains
how good to get reacquainted—
four billion year rock scored with
her passage
the fragrance of heather
Black Hills

*

Palmyra leaves. Foll. 82. 14½" by 1¼". Old, worm-eaten and injured. Good medium grantha writing. Lines five on a page. Inked. Wooden board at either end. Complete.

*

"The twisting spine of the central massif, the jagged
angular brushwork
puffy cloudlike rocks recall the—
(& that day the fog lifted, the Brecon Beacons
lifted tawny & black away in the north)
monumental landscapes of Guo Xi whose
forged signature appears on the left
edge of the painting."

*

Some nights after my final visit to the library I awoke in the pre-dawn hours, & saw the *Prajna-paramita*'s blue & silver pages in the dark space overhead, bound by their elastic cord. The apparition felt neither scary nor spectacular. Through my thoughts like lyrics to a half remembered song went a Sanskrit phrase. As I looked closer—into the nightbound space where the archaic book hung, its pages radiant with midnight indigo & its script of luminous interstellar dust—the resounding phrase becoming more audible—I realized the syllables were the manuscript itself—her voice—searching me out. The text the goddess's own body bending the bow of insight. The hunter had become the hunted. The re-searcher the one sought.

Stalking under the covers
for you

or between

*

To sew chance

"only
to discover
in their scattered arrangement"
an unexpec-
ted
beauty

*

She crept through an interstice of sleep
patient through centuries
defying the airless reading room of the India
& Oriental Offices
leather-bound catalogues heaped along
massive walls near
St. Pancras.
Pinnacles of rock & mist
volumes rising against one another
with the upward heave
of tectonic plates—
fragrance of pine the crisp scent

"Her function is purely
spiritual
it leads to the insight that
all dharmas are
empty"

*

... towards the center certain pages water damaged
where the black fabric cord passes through. The fibers
have expanded, the ink is washed out, fragments of

paper have flecked off through the centuries. The
manuscript otherwise appears in good shape…

Voice high in your throat
(kissed in the dream your russet hair)
Beloved lift
your throat up for a—

& the aged oaks reflect in the Abergavenny canal's
still waters, a red
shimmer a phone booth
hanging on the skittenish hill
incongruous on the water's
surface marvel'd & laugh'd—
(unable to read the script but learnt
unexpected
kindness from you
hand fanned out across the stomach)

*

utkantha
a cry from between two covers,
wrapt
in yellowish linen
nagas twining about they resemble
(the calligrapher
told us) tiny snakes

Mother of Buddhas out of your—

Echo out of the
text & the resonant uterus
to voice, to reveal deeps &
deep furthers

multiple texts scored on the flesh,
hunting as for something
lost geological
epochs ago
stalking between the
covers or under
    utkantha

Oh where to find you?

London // Llanellen, Wales // Boulder
11 Dec. '02 – 14 Feb. '03

MARCH CRESCENT MOON SONG

Bow-bent luminous ice peak refraction
brittle dry snow-horn Arikaree
foot squeak no moisture Kiowa pine formal purity—
And humans? humans always this
                clumsy at love?

GARY SNYDER, born in 1930 in San Francisco, spent his early years in Portland, Oregon. He attended Reed College, rooming with Lew Welch and Philip Whalen ("the first practicing poet I ever met"). His early writings, scored by studies in anthropology, folklore, and Native American thought, are equally notable for the jobs he held, including summers as a Forest Service fire lookout in the Olympic Mountains. After he lost government work due to connections with left-wing political groups, he worked in the timber industry and studied Chinese at U.C. Berkeley. He received a grant from the First Zen Institute of America to study in Kyoto, Japan, and spent most of the late '50s, '60s, and early '70s studying near Daitoku-ji. In Japan he also trained with *yamabushi*, the elusive mountain wanderers of the Womb Diamond Trail. Returning to North America, Gary published his 1974 volume *Turtle Island*—"the old-new name" for this continent—and received the Pulitzer Prize for Poetry. He is one of the leading spokespersons for the environmental movement, for bioregionalism as a practical application of studies in deep history, and for a specifically American form of Zen. Notable books of poetry include *The Back Country* (1968), *Axe Handles* (1983), the forty-year project *Mountains and Rivers Without End* (1996), and most recently *Danger on Peaks*. His prose includes the hugely influential essays of *Earth House Hold* (1969)—"Technical Notes & Queries To Fellow Dharma Revolutionaries"—and *The Practice of the Wild* (1990). He lives on the North San Juan Ridge in the foothills of the Sierra Nevada, California.

WORKING ON THE '58 WILLYS PICKUP

For Lu Yu

The year this truck was made
I sat in early morning darkness
Chanting sūtra in Kyoto,
And spent the days studying Chinese.
Chinese, Japanese, Sanskrit, French—
Joys of Dharma-scholarship
And the splendid old temples—
But learned nothing of trucks.

Now to bring sawdust
Rotten and rich
From a sawmill abandoned when I was just born
Lost in the young fir and cedar
At Bloody Run Creek
So that clay in the garden
Can be broken and tempered
And growing plants mulched to save water—
And to also haul gravel
From the old placer diggings,
To screen it and mix in the sand with the clay
Putting pebbles aside to strew on the paths
So muddy in winter—

I lie in the dusty and broken bush
Under the pickup
Already thought to be old—
Admiring its solidness, square lines,
Thinking a truck like this
would please Chairman Mao.

The rear end rebuilt and put back

With new spider gears,
Brake cylinders cleaned, the brake drums
New-turned and new brake shoes,
Taught how to do this
By friends who themselves spent
Youth with the Classics—

The garden gets better, I
Laugh in the evening
To pick up Chinese
And read about farming,
I fix truck and lock eyebrows
With tough-handed men of the past.

BREASTS

That which makes milk can't
                    help but concentrate
Out of the food of the world,
Right up to the point
                    where we suck it,
Poison, too

But the breast is a filter—
The poison stays there, in the flesh.
Heavy metals in traces
                    deadly molecules hooked up in strings
                    that men dreamed of;
Never found in the world til today.
                    (in your bosom
                    petrochemical complex
                    astray)

So we celebrate breasts
We all love to kiss them
                    —they're like philosophers!
Who hold back the bitter in mind
To let the more tasty
Wisdom slip through
                    for the little ones.
                    who can't take the poison so young.

The work that comes later
After child-raising
For the real self to be,
Is to then burn the poison away.
Flat breasts, tired bodies,
That will snap like old leather,

tough enough
for a few more good days,

And the glittering eyes,
Old mother,
Old father,

are gay.

WALKING THROUGH MYOSHIN-JI

Straight stone walks
    up lanes between mud walls

. . . the sailors who handled the ships
    from Korea and China,
the carpenters, chisels like razors,

    young monks working on *mu*,

    and the pine trees
        that surrounded this city.
        the Ancient Ones, each one
    anonymous.
        green needles,
            lumber,
                ash.

VII, 81, KYOTO

FOR CAROLE

I first saw her in the zendo
at meal time   unwrapping bowls
head forward folding back the cloth
        as a server I was kneeling
to fill three sets of bowls each time
up the line
                Her lithe leg
                proud, skeptical,
                passionate, trained
                by the
                heights   by the
                danger on peaks

REALLY THE REAL

FOR KO UN AND LEE SANG-WHA

Heading south down the freeway making the switch
from Business 80 east to the I-5 south,
watch those signs and lanes that split
duck behind the trucks, all going 75 at 10 AM
I tell Ko Un this is the road that runs from Mexico to Canada,
right past San Diego—LA—Sacramento—Medford—Portland—
  Centralia—
Seattle—Bellingham, B.C. all the way,
the new suburban projects with cement roof tiles
neatly piled on unfinished gables,
turn onto Twin Cities Road, then Franklin Road
pull in by the sweet little almost-wild Cosumnes River
right where the Mokulumne meets it,
(*umne* a Miwok suffix meaning river)
walking out on a levee trail through cattail, tule, button-brush,
small valley oaks, algae on the streams. Hardly any birds.
Lost Slough, across the road, out on the boardwalk
—can't see much, the tules all too tall. The freeway roar,
four sandhill cranes feeding, necks down, pacing slow.
Then west on Twin Cities Road til we hit the river.
Into Locke, park, walk the crowded Second Street
all the tippy buildings' second stories leaning out,
gleaming bikes—huge BMW with exotic control panel
eat at the Locke Gardens Chinese place, Ko Un's choice,
endless tape loop some dumb music, at the next table one white couple,
a guy with a beard; at another a single black woman
with two little round headed clearly super-sharp boys.
Out and down to Walnut Grove til we find road J-11 going east
over a slough or two then south on Staten Island Road. It's straight,
the fields all flat and lots of signs that say
no trespassing, no camping, no hunting, stay off the levee.

Driving along, don't see much, I had hoped, but about to give up.
Make a turn around and stand on the shoulder, glass the field:
flat farmland—fallow—flooded with water—
full of birds. Scanning the farther sections
hundreds of sandhill cranes are pacing—then,
those gurgling sandhill crane calls are coming out of the sky
in threes, twos, fives, from all directions,
circling, counter-spinning, higher and lower,
big silver bodies, long necks, dab of red on the head,
chaotic, leaderless, harmonic, playful—what are they doing?
Splendidly nowhere thousands

And back to Davis, forty miles, forty minutes
shivering to remember what's going on
just a few miles west of the 5:
in the wetlands, in the ongoing elder what you might call,
really the real, world.

(OCTOBER 2001, COSUMNES
AND STATEN ISLAND)

WAITING FOR A RIDE

Standing at the baggage passing time:
Austin Texas airport — my ride hasn't come yet.
My former wife is making websites from her home,
one son's seldom seen,
the other one and his wife have a boy and girl of their own.
My wife and stepdaughter are spending weekdays in town
so she can get to high school.
My mother ninety-six still lives alone and she's in town too,
always gets her sanity back just barely in time.
My former former wife has become a unique poet;
most of my work,
such as it is   is done.
Full moon was October second this year,
I ate a mooncake, slept out on the deck
white light beaming through the black boughs of the pine
owl hoots and rattling antlers,
Castor and Pollux rising strong
— it's good to know that the Pole Star drifts!
that even our present night sky slips away,
not that I'll see it.
Or maybe I will, much later,
some far time walking the spirit path in the sky,
that long walk of spirits—where you fall right back into the
"narrow painful passageway of the Bardo"
squeeze your little skull
and there you are again

waiting for your ride

(October 5, 2001)

COFFEE, MARKETS, BLOSSOMS

My Japanese mother-in-law
born in America
tough with brokers
a smart trader
grew up working barefoot
in the Delta, on the farm.
Doesn't like Japan.
Sits in the early morning
by the window, coffee in hand,

gazing at cherry blossoms.
Jean Koda
needing no poem.

NO SHADOW

My friend Deane took me into the Yuba Goldfields. That's at the lower Yuba River outflow where it enters the Sacramento valley flatlands, a mile-wide stretch between grass and blue oak meadows. It goes on for ten miles. Here's where the mining tailings got dropped off by the wandering riverbed of the 1870s — forty miles downstream from where the giant hoses washed them off Sierra slopes.

We were walking on blue lupine-covered rounded hundred-foot gravel hills til we stood over the springtime rush of water. Watched a female osprey hunting along the main river channel. Her flight shot up, down, all sides, suddenly fell feet first into the river and emerged with a fish. Maybe fooling the fish by zigzagging, so — no hawk shadow. Carole said later, that's like trying to do zazen without your self entering into it.

Standing on a gravel hill by the lower Yuba
can see down west a giant airforce cargo plane from Beale
hang-gliding down to land
strangely slow over the tumbled dredged-out goldfields
— practice run
shadow of a cargo jet — soon gone

no-shadow of an osprey

still here

ARTHUR SZE

ARTHUR SZE was born in New York City in 1950. A second generation Chinese American, he attended the University of California at Berkeley where he studied classical Chinese. Of contemporary American poets his use of the image is perhaps the most insistently reminiscent of the legendary T'ang and Sung Dynasty masters, though the manner in which he juxtaposes images is decisively postmodern. This gives his poetry a flavor that feels deeply invested in the poetries associated with Ch'an Buddhism, yet precisely contemporary. In *The Best American Poetry of 2004* he wrote of his included poem, "...the impulse to the poem is to close one's eyes in order to see." Arthur is the recipient of numerous literary awards including a Guggenheim Fellowship, a Lannan Literary Award, three awards from the Witter Bynner Foundation, and a Lila Wallace-Reader's Digest Grant. Two recent collections from Sam Hamill's Copper Canyon Press present his distinctive work: *The Redshifting Web: Poems 1970–1998* and *Archipelago*. From the time of his studies at Berkeley he has carefully worked at translating Chinese poetry, both classical (T'an Chien, Li Po, Wang Wei, Li Ch'ing Chiao) and of recent centuries. These have now been collected in *The Silk Dragon: Translations from the Chinese,* also Copper Canyon Press. His own poetry has been translated into Chinese, Italian, and Turkish. Arthur lives just north of Santa Fe near the old pueblo of Pojoaque with his wife, the poet Carole Moldaw, and is a professor of creative writing at the Institute of American Indian Arts.

BEFORE SUNRISE

The myriad unfolds from a progression of strokes—
one, ice, corpse, hair, jade, tiger.

Unlocking a gate along a barbed wire fence,
I notice beer cans and branches in the acequia.

There are no white pear blossoms by the gate,
no red poppies blooming in the yard,

no *Lepiota naucina* clustered by the walk,
but—bean, gold—there's the intricacy of a moment

when—wind, three-legged incense cauldron—
I begin to walk through a field with cow pies

toward the Pojoaque River, sense deer, *yellow,* rat.
I step through water, go up the arroyo, find

a dark green magpie feather. This is a time
when—blood in my piss, ache in nose and teeth—

I sense tortoise, flute where there is no sound,
wake to human bones carved and strung into a loose apron.

SOLSTICE QUIPU

Hong Kong 87, New York 84;
he glances at isobars on the weather map;

ashes accumulate at the tip of an incense stick;

mosquitoes are hatching near the Arctic Circle;

300,000 acres in Arizona scorched or aflame;

the aroma of *genmai* tea from a teapot with no lid;

where is the Long March now?
And Lin Biao—so what if
he salivated behind a one-way mirror at naked women?

lobstermen color code their buoys;

string sandals number knotted mine the gold of the output of s on—
though things are not yet in their places,
the truth sears his fingertips:

the output of gold mines,
the number of sandals knotted on string;

orange globe of sun refracted through haze;

a two-year-old gasps at hummingbirds lying on a porch;

he observes a torn screen, nods
male and *female, black-chinned*;
spells the iridescent gorget of spring.

THERMODYNAMICS

He tips hot water into a cup, stirs the powdered
Ling Chih mushroom, hands it to you. You observe
black specks swirling in the inky tonic: sip,
shudder, sip. It is supposed to treat neurasthenia,
dizziness, insomnia, high serum cholesterol,
coronary disease, rhinitis, asthma, duodenal ulcers,
boost the immune system. You scan the room,
catch crescendos and decrescendos to the flute
music on the stand, pick out the first character,
"Spring," written in official script on a scroll—
Warring States bronze mirrors lined up on stands.
You pick up the last strands of glistening jellyfish,
note speckled tracks of grease on the platter,
feel as if you are jostled in a small airplane
as it descends into cumulus clouds. In Beijing
a couple wanted to thank him for arranging
financial sponsorship of their son in America;
under the table, she rubbed her leg against his
and whispered she had tomorrow off from work;
but *tomorrow, lust, betrayal, delight, yesterday,*
ardor, scorn, forgiveness are music from empty holes,
and you wonder if the haphazard course of a life
follows a fundamental equation in thermodynamics.
He pulls Styrofoam out of a box and reveals
a two-foot-high human figure from the tomb of
the Third Han Emperor; the face and trunk are intact,
though arms and hands are gone. He bequeaths
it to you, though requests that you pass it on
someday to a museum. You nod, sip the cool tonic,
down a few last black specks at the bottom of the cup.

INFLORESCENCE

1

Go sway on a suspension bridge over a gorge;
you do not ponder the beauty of an azure
lotus-shaped wine-warming bowl with five
spurs the size of sesame seeds at the base,
but, instead, inhale the cool mist sliding
over pines, making the white boulders below
disappear and reappear. This is how you
become absent to pancakes smoking on a griddle—
pricked once in thought, you are pinned,
singed back to the watery splendor of the hour:
wisteria leaves thin to transparency on the porch;
a girl relaxes on horseback in the field
while sunlight stipples her neck. You smile,
catch the aroma of pumpkin seed in the oven,
exult at the airy, spun filaments of clouds.
Before there was above and below, who was there
to query? One marks a bloody trail in water
from a harpooned narwhal, dreams of clustered
igloos lit by seal oil. You flicker, nod:
what one has is steeped in oil, wicked into flame.

2

Whisked back and forth,
a fly
drops on water;

  a floating narwhal
  resembles a human corpse;

screwdrivers, pliers, CDs,
a duct-taped taillight
strewn in the grass;

  running my tongue
  along your nape;

singed by
apple leaves
on the windshield;

  smooth black stones
  in a glass bowl;

where the mind
that is
no-mind is;

  fingertips
  on a frosted pane.

3

A shrinking loop becomes a noose: at the airport
a Choctaw writer scrawls a few words to his wife,
creases the paper, fires a slug into his chest.
A woman smokes, ruminates on a blank canvas
she does not yet know will remain blank.
I push hoops into the dirt, prop up a few
tomato branches: a single Black Krim has reseeded
from last summer. I uproot some weeds, toss them,
but, in thought, recoil from flies on a squirrel;
raise a lid to a plastic barrel: find hamburger
wrappers, stomped soda cans; notice irregular bits
of white glass near where I vacuum my car.
As a red snake snags its epidermis, the mind snags,
molts from inside out. Although sand plunges
in an hourglass—soon the last white particles
will vanish from the top—I ache for a second,
sulfur butterfly pinned our black paper, to stop:
but, eelgrass in tidal water, I catch the scent
of tomato leaves on my hands, swing palms near
a horse's head: flies flit and land, flit and reland.

4

Incise the beginning and end to all motion;

q w e r t y u i o p, in a line above your fingertips;

align river stones for a walkway;

halt at clusters of notes from swinging copper-green wind chimes;

shovel twigs and beer cans out of a ditch;

this wave of pollen light on your face is the end of summer;

rub Maximilian sunflower petals with your hands;

sniff red silk pine-bark patterned gauze unearthed out of a tomb;

splay juniper with an ax;

water brims her eyes when you stroke her wrist;

observe a *Bombyx mori* consume mulberry leaves for seven days;

ponder a missing shade of blue;

sweat when you eat that Chimayo chile stuffed with lamb;

pinch off basil flowers;

graze patches of faint aquamarine paint on a bathroom door;

spasm;

revolve a polygon inside a circle;

squint up at a magpie nest in the cottonwood branches;

survey a skater's mark left in the ice in executing a half-turn;

inscribe the beginning and end to all motion.

5

In the zero sunlight a man at a traffic light
waving today's newspaper becomes a man
who, wiping windshields at night in a drizzle
as cars come off the Brooklyn Bridge,
opens his hands. Behind your parked car,
you stoop to peruse a speckled brown egg
on the gravel, glance up to sight a ring-tailed
lemur on a branch. Though no red-winged
blackbirds nest in the cattails this summer,
though someone has tried to drain the pond
into a nearby acequia, there is nothing
to drain, and you nod, curse, laugh—
you have nothing, everything in mind.
When I run my fingers between your fingers,
when we wet river wet through white Embudo water,
the hush is a shocked stillness: a black
bug stretches the skin of water and circles out.
As moonlight slants through the screen door,
I mark the span of our lives suspended
over the undulating scritch scratch of crickets.

6

I sip warm wine out of a sky-blue bowl
flecked with agate crystals in the glaze,

press my eyes, squint at walruses on an ice floe.
When you step on stones in plover formation

and enter a tea garden—shift the rhythm
of your body, mind; admire the slender

splayed arc of branches, singed maple leaves
scattered on gravel—you arrive at the cusp

where you push open a blue-planked door,
inhale the aroma of a miniature calla lily

in an oblong vase, bend over a brass trashcan
to find a cluster of ants that must have

dropped from the ceiling and, disoriented, died.
And as the configuration at dusk of flaring

willow leaves on the skylight becomes minnows
in water, what is above becomes what is below.

And as what appears up close to be a line
becomes by air, the arc of a circle,

I smell your hair in my hands, coalesce
warmth and light of seal oil lamps into flame.

7

A woman and an instructor skydive over an island;
their parachutes fail, and they plunge into a yard,
barely missing someone snipping morning glories.
How long did they freefall before they knew
the end? We stare at Dungenness crab shells strewn
across the table, pull cupcakes out of the oven,
and, smoothing icing on them to the rhythm of
African drumming, sizzle along a cusp of dream.
Who knows what the Coal Sack in the Milky Way is?
Who cares that the Eta Carinae Nebula is about
9,000 light-years distant? A moment in the body
is beauty's memento mori: when I rake gravel in
a courtyard, or sweep apricot leaves off a deck,
I know an inexorable inflorescence in May sunshine;
watch a man compose a flower arrangement
in Tokyo using polychrome Acoma pots. And as
a narwhal tusk pokes out of a hole in the ice,
as a thumbprint momentarily forms in thawing frost
on a pane, we heat a precarious splendor,
inscribe the end and beginning to all motion.

IN THE LIVING ROOM

I turn this green hexagonal tile with
a blue dragonfly, but what is it I am turning?
The vertical scroll on the far wall

has seven characters that roughly translate,
"The sun's reflection on the Yangtze River
in ten thousand miles of gold." A Japanese

calligrapher drew these Chinese characters
in the 1890s, but who knows the circumstances
of the event? I graze the crackled paper,

recognize a moment ready to scrape into flame;
gaze at ceiling beams from Las Trampas,
at Peñasco floorboards softened with lye.

Along the wall on a pedestal, a gold-leafed
male and female figure join in sexual embrace.
Hours earlier, my hands held your hips,

your breasts brushed my chest. I close
my eyes, feel how in the circumference
of a circle the beginning and end have no end.

NATHANIEL TARN

BORN IN 1928 in Paris, Nathaniel Tarn grew up in France and Belgium, established himself as a poet and editor in the U.K., then moved permanently to the United States in 1967. He attended Cambridge, the Sorbonne, and the London School of Economics, with studies in anthropology and Asian cultures. Tarn conducted early field work in Guatemala from 1952–53, and Burma from 1958–59. In Burma he gathered material for the first substantial study of Burmese Buddhism, *Sangha & State in Burma: A Study of Monastic Sectarianism & Leadership.* He sat zazen at Daitoku-ji temple in Kyoto, 1961. Tarn has thus led two intertwined careers: anthropologist and poet. In London he helped found Cape Editions, an international and multidisciplinary series of small books, and Cape Goliard, which published Charles Olson, Robert Duncan, Louis Zukofsky, William S. Burroughs, and other Americans in the U.K. He has 35 books and chapbooks of his own. Significant titles include *The Beautiful Contradictions, Lyrics for the Bride of God,* and *Seeing America First.* In 1991 University of New Mexico Press released *Views from the Weaving Mountain: Selected Essays in Poetics & Anthropology.* Tarn has published many translations (his Pablo Neruda the most acclaimed), and been associated with the "ethnopoetics" movement since its beginnings in the 1960s, "working at the translation of archaic, tribal, ethnic, and national minority literatures to broaden the scope of poetic understanding beyond the horizon of strictly national literatures." *Selected Poems 1950–2000* came out from University Press of New England in 2002. He works as an independent scholar and practitioner, living outside Santa Fe with his wife Janet Rodney.

HEARING ABOUT THE VIRTUAL DESTRUCTION OF PAIN

"Dear friend of my pain" he told himself, "since I
can recollect myself with the help you give me,
each moment realize where — held to the threads
of path and carriage for that path" — thus what
the world spends most time losing he would keep
who had, his whole existence tried to hide away
from any form of it: hurt, loss, or, even, gain
(for gain would signalize a loss of *everything*)
and yet he would still face it as present moves
into the future . . . in the huge fields of heaven
they'd heard about that evening, imperial Tibet
lay on the ground — ruins in the research films
appearing like abolished backdrops in a theater
lacking even the use of ruins. From boyhood on,
out of Kingdon Ward's "*In the Blue Poppy Land,*"
he'd hunt rare orchids and these monasteries —
Now the most crucifying pain he'd ever suffered
wrenching shoulder from socket each time he sat
rose or did anything but lie (flat on his back)
would flash like a new lucifer in the human sky
whenever he bent attention back, his inner eye,
day on day, in any kind of weather of the mind.

THE FIRST ZEN ABBESS OF AMERICA

That morning, while driving to his job,
he had burst out in a sudden, loud wail
for all creatures suffering the world—
which meant primarily his people—then
like sobs spreading out around his body
to the world's rim, all the beings also
he couldn't know. "The hurt" he sighed,
"for those I hurt so long ago back home
and have been in agony over ever since,
for this one destroying me now, for one
she'd pain if she decides she won't go,
for this one I hurt by throwing her out
for hurting me." World history morning:
"how intolerably we are part of a circle
of those who give and take pain at this
one time. And, each time, is there hope
one will break the circle and move out,
move all of us out toward calm? Perhaps
it will be a woman whose deep-read eyes
tune more wisely day by day to her fate
knowing she breaks me—not wishing it."

RETREAT TOWARD THE SPRING

While they sit and walk in alternation, their glance cast down, the only stirring from the external world he'll allow himself is a flare from her olive skirt. Noises of the alley outside: sunday loafers passing, excited talk, a radio at full tilt, far off a siren, ambulance sounding so sweet for a change, as if pain were singing in joy far away young and affectionate. Alternation of silence and chanting, the harmonizing sometimes very loud. Then: swift cataract of silence within whose pool only a bird warbles, as in a world only he crowds. The dead watch them in silence: from their planets, are in such close touch, so intimate, woven into all life: they know them all so well (the living) there is no reason ever to manifest. Need to come to that which will come to you so flying and so *entirely*? As knees cramp, pain spreads up the spine, as the silent forms almost break with aching, breath coming shorter, turning to sobs almost, an exquisite smell of roast veal wafts down from the outer street into the door of the monastery. It is five o'clock.

A MAN WHOSE NAME RHYMES WITH PEACE

On his return, he finds from the man rhyming peace
a last book on what a Buddha really taught, plus a
death letter. A doctor, put out, said four months.
It suits me fine, he said. The doctor, embarrassed,
talked pains and pills. It suits me fine, he said.
An undertaker, embarrassed, told to recall his fee,
our man of peace witnessed his own certificate. No
more vivacious letter had ever been penned. As one
grows older, he thought, one is inhabited more and
more by more people inside one. They come forth at
odd moments of day or night to visit, face sharper
than they had had in life. One becomes a house for
an inner empire of death, carrying that whole race
into the future. It's hard to grasp that everyone,
everyone here, right now, in millions will one day
no longer be. Except in that carrying, and even it
stops. One day, unready for the most part — you go
inside yourself and, suddenly, have friends again,
all leaning out of their home with welcoming hands
and you go in, doubtless — in and take your place,
where you've always belonged and always conquered.

AS IF THERE WERE ANY MATTER

"And how is it we think we make the world move
and bring up the sun at dawn, go down with it,
at night, when it loses its flesh in the sea?"
he asked, as leaves fell in a blaze — all over
the garden floor — and, for once, they watched
at peace without doing anything in particular:
"How can we see something so special about us,
the world has to stop, pay attention, turn its
collective smile to us, welcome us to a podium
leave us hour after hour yacking at this smile
which never tires, nor sorrows, never draws to
any end but sustains us fully a whole breath?"
Facing that wall on which there are no leaves,
cut with graffiti of disaster etched in darker
character looking through the wall to the sea:
day waves one similar to another or very close
washing dearth like grease to warm sun's bones
as he lies at dusk ("poor, small father sun!")
listening for the noise of leaves falling down
scratching like ghosts round the broken house,
he marvels, he wonders, asks sky over and over
for the original face of our questions or font
of talk as if our sun were justicer to others.

THE HEART STUMBLES IN DARKNESS

Anxious at every moment of his life, without fail.
Each time, as if he were on the brink of an abyss.
At every moment, lapsing a step into the darkness.
That cavern where consciousness seems to vegetate,
a hollow prison full of dark steps, trip and fall.
"If I could only bury my face in her body — invade
her, hang out for some time as in the sacred river
of salvation bathed in waters as cool as their own
definition, come out on the other side of herself,
like the word having its being in the world, *then*,
I could know that single moment free of it, again,
that moment would spread out everywhere and assume
all time, to home in purified, recovered, reborn."
Little but the week has gone by in his divine city
where men still hear of salvation; the narcissi on
his desk are still pungent and send him, all night
messages of self-pleasure — yet, already he misses
her odors where she sits on the world and makes it
human for him to adopt, be reborn into, as if from
a lifelong death, fear, that companion at his side
walking with deliberate slowness, the black beast,
in pace with him, stalling the outcome of the sun.

RECOLLECTIONS OF BEING

Cloud around tree outside window, in
which, at sudden motion of the mind,
all is contained again. Not to be here —
but there, in cloud, and to be there
as being here of which, in other wise,
there's no conception. Birds, joyed at
feeder, raven within my satiation,
each one his one and only mask, and yet
also all others' being and my own. Tree's
self at home in cloud, cloud in high sky,
to furthest worlds, all single dwelling
of this unity. Forgotten now forgetting, no
more the absent-minded in full preoccupation
with the ten thousand things, each separate,
each needing its own space and unique memory.
Years seem to have gone by in this forgetting.
Do thousand lives have to be wasted now
to sharpen this one life? But all the lives
return again into the picture as sun wills me
to wither down to a last flare of love. Day
darkens. The oldsome window overglows my birds.

KLUANE, THE YUKON

a nostalgia, for Tsetaeva.

Only the van's half inch of steel
between us and the universe outside:
swigging our vodka to the bottle's floor
we loved in a silent storm of stars,
waters and maps.

At dawn, the ice shivered like music,
playing its xylophones. Teeth clamped,
we washed in ice. Then drove into a North
yearning to soak up every nation's freshness
in its granite heart.

Ravens, sunned dry, less hoarse by now,
pointed us up to what had been
a one-time arm of Rus — its distant reach
clawing at memories of shattered childhoods:
pogroms, shards, massacres.

"What shall I do, singer and first-born,
with all immensity in such a measured world?"

This land was once owned by itself
with its own natives.
When this nation, which had brooked its Europe,
became America —
it was essential that the talk continue.
The talk did not.

Whelmed, we looked out at spaces wide
as the betrothal of the world and ocean.

CHASE TWICHELL

CHASE TWICHELL was born in 1950, growing up in New Haven, Connecticut and the Adirondack Mountains of northern New York State. She attended Trinity College, then received an M.F.A. from the University of Iowa Writer's Workshop in 1976. She spent a decade working as a letterpress printer, typesetter, and book designer, following which she taught at various colleges including Princeton University from 1990 until 1999. In 1999 she left Princeton and quit teaching to found Ausable Press, a not-for-profit publisher of contemporary poetry. From 1995–2001 Chase studied with John Daido Loori at Zen Mountain Monastery in upstate New York. Recipient of many grants and awards, including a Guggenheim Memorial Foundation Fellowship and two from the National Endowment for the Arts, she has published five books of poetry, most recently *The Snow Watcher.* She is co-editor of *The Practice of Poetry: Writing Exercises From Poets Who Teach. The Lover of God*, translations (with Bengali scholar Tony K. Stewart) of a volume of poetry by the Nobel Prize winner Rabindrinath Tagore, came out from Sam Hamill's Copper Canyon Press in 2004; a new book of poems, *Dog Language*, will be forthcoming in 2005, also from Copper Canyon. Chase lives in the Adirondacks, in "the last significant wilderness east of the Rockies," with her husband, the novelist Russell Banks.

THE PAPER RIVER

The most beloved body
of my childhood was Johns Brook,
its bed of ancient broken pears,
icy libations pouring
over them for centuries.
Through the leaky oval mask
I entered its alcoves and grand halls,
its precincts of green-brown light,
the light of my infant thinking.
In the minnow-bright roar
I saw the place where life and art
meet underwater stone to stone,
with the sunken treasure and trash.
The sound of the brook
was the sound of the house,
the pools of the kitchen and bedrooms.
A galaxy away it would still be
the background of my sleep.

Clouds came down to earth,
great gloomy rooms among the trees,
dark rooms of the brook,
church of deep pools.
As soon as you entered
you were wholly alone in it,
all sinewy ladders
and gray stairs, stones magnified,
and the sidelong trout,
all gone now,
rainbows and brookies,
one big one per pool,
gills like fresh cuts.

I dove into the flume's mystery,
no place you could touch bottom
or see all the way down in
because half at least
was always in shadow.
It was like learning a room
by carrying a candle
corner to corner,
looking for God to see if He too
was awake and listening
to the river crumpling and erasing,
enforcing its laws.
I found a cold, an oblique god
who commanded me to answer
all my questions by myself.

The human mind
is also a beautiful river,
full of driftwood and detritus,
bones hung with trinkets,
scant beaches more stones than sand.
And up on the hills it's the wind
touching the juniper spurned
by the cows, its thistle sharpness,
and the fawn's hoof
left by coyotes,
in their scat.

TOPIARY ROOSTER

Five-thirty on a summer afternoon,
Mom's sharpening a knife.
Dad comes in like a river current,
a hard little swirl around him
like muscles but of the air.
The first cork's been pulled,
teepee of kindling built in the grill.
Tonight it's about the rooster again,
Mom's topiary beheaded by Dad
because all these years
he thought that end was the tail.
I'm working on the conversion
of my handwriting from yarn
to razor wire, making a list of words
that seem to have inner lives:
marinade, carbon steel.
Eliza's there beside me, staging
a wedding of the pepper to the salt.

Some two-cycle machine starts up
in the valley, bringing back the scream
and smell of burned wood from his saw,
the lathe whining spirals to the floor.
She'd be shut up in their bedroom,
mid-afternoon, hardly any sound
but the breath said it was weeping.
Did I already have my own
sadness apart from hers?
One that might run together
with a rivulet of hers?
I think so, but she didn't want
to touch sorrows with me.

She lay waiting for some psychic
match to strike her life back to the way
it was supposed to be,
with a closet full of dresses
not yet imagined,
and late sun agleam
on the scotch-colored
hills of Connecticut.

My mind goes up into the high pines
and sits among the crows.
I can hear Harry Belafonte singing
Come back Liza, Come back girl,
which always made my sister cry.
How easily that song is put out
by a swish of wind!
Still, I stay up there for a while
above the house as it was then,
painted to match the granite
on which it was built,
with lichen-colored trim,
and two kids watching their mother
sharpen her long-bladed shears,
then continue to snip sway
at the rooster, lush and fully formed,
the way he should have been.

Don't go back, say the crows.
Stay here in the gold opening
left by the storm, quick storm,
big truck passing on the highway,
gone now behind the washed and dazzling clouds.

Let all the words go.
They come from elsewhere
and long ago, are immigrants here.
They should return to their faraway homes.
They should fly up to city balconies
and preen there,
or land like a big shadow on the cornfield,
and pick among the stalks.

TUTELAGE

Stone ruins of a monastery,
door still standing,
starving horse tied to a tree.
My dog is lost—I call
but no one comes.
I dream this repeatedly.

When the student is ready,
the teacher appears.
And if the student is not?
Is still a child?
Words in a red notebook,
not hymns. I never chose
my teachers or their gods,
all of them peering down
over the pall of Modern Europe,
Algebra's barbed wire,
the barking (in French) of Monsieur.
Heart-to-hearts concerning
discipline and striving.
Heartless tests.
Surrogate family. What a laugh.
Bye-bye, the whole lot of you.

Fair are the meadows,
fairer still the woodlands—
words and woodlands
briefly simultaneous—
maybe *that* was God?
And childhood?
A wind blew through it,
stealing shingles,

breaking branches,
not saying thank you,
not saying goodbye.

I will not speak of my first tutor.
He was my tutor and no one else's.
I dedicate this poem to the flies
that came to the wound.

MARIJUANA

Stoned by noon, I'd take the trail
that runs along the X River
in the State of Y, summer of '69,
crows' black ruckus overhead.
I'd wade through the ferns' sound
of vanishing to the almost-invisible ledge,
stark basin canted out to the southwest:
sheltered, good drainage,
full sun, remote, state land.
You could smell the blacker, foreign green
from a long way off when it rained,
incense-grade floral, the ripening spoils,
then pang of wood smoke,
antiseptic pitch and balsam,
scents cut like initials in a beech,
then cold that kills the world for a while,
puts it under, then wakes it up
again in spring when it's still tired.
I woke from its anesthesia
wanting the tight buds of my loneliness
to swell and split, not die in waiting.
It was why I rushed through everything,
why I tore away at the perpetual gauze
between me and the stinging world,
its starlight and resins,
new muscle married to smoke and tar,
just wedding the world for a while.
About to divorce it, too,
to marry some other smoke and tar.

On snow shoes in falling snow,
we lugged peat, manure,

and greensand a mile up there,
alfalfa meal, spent hops.
The clones bronzed, hairy and sticky,
and a week before frost we'd slice
the dirt around them with a bread knife,
which gave the dope
a little extra turpentine.
Weed, reefer, smoke—
it was one of life's perfumes.
Sometimes its flower opens
on a city street, gray petals,
phantom musk dispersing.
The other day I caught myself
checking the matches to see
if all the dead ones faced backwards.
They did. It's an old habit,
a watchfulness over disorder,
an anxiety keeping its distance
like a feral dog that won't touch
anything kindness touched.

Sleeping out on the high ledges
on a bed of blueberries dwarfed
by wind and springy beneath the blankets,
we'd watch for meteors and talk till dawn,
gazing toward the pinnacle in the distance,
pyramid to the everlasting glory
of Never Enough, not far below us
in his tomb, asleep in the granite chill
with the bones of his faithful animals.

Could this be the pinnacle?
To be slumming back there
buoyant on the same old
wave just breaking,
now the wave of words, the liftoff?
I'm still cracking open the robin's egg

to see the yellow heart, the glue.
A pinnacle is a fulcrum,
a scale. And now that it's tipped,
I can look back through the ghost
of self-consciousness to its embryo,
first the tomboy,
then the chick in a deerskin skirt,
the first breaking of the spirit,
the heart's deflowerment.

Caw, caw, a crow wants to nip
the memory in the bud,
the ember of the mind
as it was before it tasted
the dark meat of the world.
But I can call it back—
the match's sulphur spurt,
its petals of carbon and tar,
a flash of mind, a memory:
how after each deflowerment,
I became the flower.

THE QUALITY OF STRIVING

My war pits sleep's enthrallments
against those of consciousness.
I often encounter a miniature
localized tiredness,
droopy yellow flag marking
a tree to come down.
Next second I'm setting out to master
the subspecies of all conifers
in the region and the first five hundred
Latin vocabulary flashcards.

If you think northern spring
is more beautiful than spring in the south,
then on some level you understand
that I write by the light of the secret
Protestant pride in asceticism,
the most seductive Buddha of all.

Eye-catching as a dog on a chain,
tough-muscled, brash,
talking fifty-fifty words/harmonica,
Bob Dylan let himself as an old man
sit in on the songs.
I want words half zendo,
half casino, like his,
cruder and more fluent than this,
with a swelling inevitability about them,
an itch, the way a bud must itch
before it breaks.

MY LISTENER

When hope forms a bud of prayer,
who picks it?
Words in all languages
yearn toward the stars,
confessing and beseeching.

I talk to a masculine higher power
half god, half human.
When he sits calm and golden,
spine straight as the Buddha's,
my own spine yearns upward
toward the clean sky of his face.
But when he lounges
on the butcher's throne
setting wars on fire from afar,
then hunting in the gutted,
rotting lands, he's my enemy, the one
who lifted my father from the cradle
in his claws so many years ago,
then let him fall,
a stick of driftwood someone saved,
provenance unknown.

Dad waits for cocktail hour,
cookies and juice,
repeating the word "voice-mail" to himself,
anxious about the new technologies,
the FAX and the microwave.
At night in his stainless crib,
he addresses
the One Who Knows Everything
yet does nothing, who ekes out

a bright fistful of candies
to keep the game alive
while the child prays for death,
shaking the safety rails.

When my Listener shows me his ribs
all my austerities gather around me,
earnest and gray, and I vow
to make myself invisible,
possessionless,
a servant of the world.
But he's only a demi-god,
and jealous. He commands me
to meet him in private.
I tell him the truth insofar
as I know it. He says nothing.
We always meet in private.
When he whips his starving flocks
I'm there alone with him.

LET'S TALK

Let's talk about his death,
right now in progress,
and about the beebees
the angry child put in his milk,
her silence as he swallowed them.
Now she remembers it
and he has no memory,
so it's her possession now.
She can give it away or use it all up.
She has not yet finished using it.

CECILIA VICUÑA

BORN IN 1948 AND RAISED in Santiago de Chile, Cecilia Vicuña is a painter, installation artist, and poet. She has lived as an exile since the early 1970s when Salvador Allende, Chile's elected president, was overthrown in a military coup. She attended the Slade School of Fine Arts, University College, London, where in 1971 she received a M.F.A., and was a founding member of Artists for Democracy. From 1975–80 she lived in Bogota, working on theater and music, and traveling through the Amazon Basin, Columbia, and Venezuela to read poetry, teach workshops, and lecture on the Chilean struggle. In 1980 she moved to New York City, but returns for long periods to South America to work. Much of her poetry alludes to traditions of the Inca, who developed in pre-Conquest times a writing system called *quipu,* which used knots on a cord. Two of Cecilia's books refer to this—*Word & Thread* and *Unraveling Words & the Weaving of Water*, the latter translated into English by Eliot Weinberger and Suzanne Jill Levine. Her portable artworks and small installations—she calls them *precarios*—often take place outdoors using locally found material. She has had exhibitions at the Royal Botanic Gardens, Edinburgh, in Berkeley, London, Bogota, and Santiago. From an early age she studied Hindu, Buddhist, and Taoist texts; her books weave frequent quotations from these texts into her poetry. In 1997 Wesleyan University Press published a dual volume, *Quipoem* by Cecilia Vicuña, and *The Precarious: The Art and Poetry of Cecilia Vicuña*, edited by M. Catherine de Zegher.

THE SHADOW OF A LOOM

I set a loom in the street
Looming above
A puddle of rain.

"We are the thread"
says she
"To weave is to speak"

Thread in the air
Cloud in the mud

UNTITLED

And if I devoted my life
to one of its feathers
to living its nature
being it understanding it
until the end

Reaching a time
when my acts
are the thousand
tiny ribs of the feather
and my silence
the humming the whispering
of wind in the feather
and my thoughts
quick sharp precise
as the non-thoughts
of the feather

TRANSLATED BY ELIOT WEINBERGER

WITH A LITTLE NOTEBOOK AT THE MET

Talisman

Would say:
        "writing to be used in the body"
like a talisman
        "the heart of the one who wears it"
the body already a writing
of arteries and veins
travelling
without end

Thuluth

Neja the form
nema the weft

My lines
have turned into
serpents
and living beings
coiling
into each other
their storm

Kufic Writing

Says:

"In a Kufic inscription the square grid
contains the attributes of god."

The body
twisting

speckled
shadow

a grained
shadowing

Backstitch
on the bias

Neither tone
nor thread
in stead
its sounding.

Linen

Threadiness
of thread

Umbilic
Umbra

The line
is born
from linen

The mother
from the son

TRANSLATED BY ROSA ALCALÁ

FABLES OF THE BEGINNING AND REMAINS OF THE ORIGIN

the great Expanse
in a tone Italic
of both worlds

EMILY DICKINSON

O pre-pensamento é o passado imediato do instante.

CLARICE LISPECTOR

Silence
turns the page
the poem begins
alba del habla, the dawn of speech.

alquimia del nombre alchemy of names
el instan
palabra fantasma
sin abrevar
trans mutation
of being.

"The soul co-authors the instant" Humberto Giannini says.

Time undone by the instant!

A *continuum* contradicted by name, time is "tem": to cut.

An instant is present,
it "stands,"
a filament of *sta,* a state of being, *stamen,*
a thread in a warp,
a web in ecstasy.

"Being" is a compound of three forms: "to grow," "to set in motion"
and "yes, it may be so."
To be not an *estar,* but a way of being.

Hay que acompañar el hilo, "you have to accompany the thread"
Don Pablo says, to pull and let go at once.

Awakening, the Buddha said: too loose it won't sing, too tight it will snap.

Awareness awakens the thread?

In awake is *awak,* the Quechua "who weaves."
A way to awaken or to leave?

Time awakens inside words.

Awayo
mi
away!

Voy a tejer
mis tres
lenguas away.

Una lengua ve en la otra el interior del estar.

El poema se desvanece en el vórtice entre las dos.

Hedda Sterne said: "Art is not in the object, nor in the eye of the beholder,
but in the meeting of both. This is the ambrosia that feeds the gods."

A word is a non-place for the encounter to take "place."

A continuous displacement, a field of "con," togetherness.

A word disappears, the connection remains.

Hear the image? See the sound? The crossing performed?

Language: an enlightened form.

Oir la música de las cuerdas en tensión, la intención.

Let the fable begin:

El comienzo es el *com,* "with" in the beginning.

Turning with the stars.

A "uni verse" wants to *con* verse.

"Verse," to turn.

Galaxies and blood
Fingerprint whorls,
breath and sound.

Ibn Arabi dreamt he made love to the stars.

In this observatory words are stars,
the night sky I see,
and language, the spinner's view.

Is the spinner spun?

Cosmic fart, little gas?

Dialogar con lo que no es palabra al interior de las palabras crea la unión.

Opening words I arrived at no word.

A moment of trance where transformation begins:
silence to sound, and back.

An empty space within words where commingling occurs.

Abriendo palabras llegué a una inmensidad.

Our common being:Language, el ser de todos in speech.

Una línea de fuerza que se acrecienta con nuestro pasar. Algo que vive en la lengua toda y emerge como el llamado de un ser.

To hear its hum, a tongue within tongues.

"Self" is "same", it says,
at once separate and not divisible from the whole.

"You and I are the same" it says,
our difference, a sound, tu per son.

> "Sounding the ten thousand things differently, so each becomes itself according to itself alone—who could make such music?"

Chuang Tzu, The Inner Chapters
translated by David Hinton

Per haps, *in di vi dual* says
un divided dual attention
un divided dual belonging
to itself and the whole at once.

Dis solve into union it says.
You will always be longing

my heart is what is not me
Antonin Artaud

Corazón del momento, el estar.

Corazón del tiempo, el instan.

imán del gen nido del son

La lengua es la memoria de la especie, its po-ethical code,
a common ode.
A bond, as in *yuga, el juguito e'la unión,* yuxta posición.

Con jugate, not sub jugate.

"Justice" began as a ritual form, an exchange.

O así lo veía mi corazón embelesado en la con templación,
the temple of con
sciousness
the fulcrum of change.

A possibility contained in the name, a pre verbal form becoming "com":
the handiwork of peace, the search for a common ground,

join with, mutually comic, c o l l e c t i v e l y.

En el "con" nacía el relato de una relación.

To carry back is to relate
a flowing of milk: time
becomes language and love,
a grammar contained in *amma.*
el amor que congrega
dice el guaraní

Una *gramma*tica fluía de la mama a la *gramma*:
la leche manando, la lengua y el trans del
instan.

Hipnótico manar
the music of am
El am
del am
or

no una idea abstracta
si no
una con
ti nui
dad.

Migrar y migrar y llegar al interior del estar.

We are only exiled from the inner estar.

Love in the genes, if it fails
We will produce no sane man again

George Oppen

THIRST

Thirst
is
the
life
of
the
spring.

TRANS. BY ROSA ALCALÁ

ELIOT WEINBERGER

ELIOT WEINBERGER has become one of the most internationally recognized writers of North America due to his translations, his controversial literary and political writings, and his astute editing. He has traveled extensively in India with his wife, Nina Sobin, a fine-art photographer, and in recent years become a principal carrier of literary news between Mexico and the United States. His books of essays include *Works on Paper*, *Outside Stories*, *Written Reaction*, *Karmic Traces*, and a recent collection of political articles, *9/12*. The author of an indispensable study of Chinese poetry translation, and translation in general, *19 Ways of Looking at Wang Wei*, he is the translator of *Unlock* by the exiled poet Bei Dao, and editor of *The New Directions Anthology of Classical Chinese Poetry*. He edited an anthology, *American Poetry Since 1950: Innovators & Outsiders*, which was published to much acclaim in a somewhat different, Spanish language edition in Mexico. His many translations of the work of Octavio Paz include the *Collected Poems 1957–1987*, *In Light of India*, and *Sunstone*. Among his other translations are Vicente Huidobro's *Altazor*, Xavier Villaurrutia's *Nostalgia for Death*, and Jorge Luis Borges' *Seven Nights* and *Selected Non-Fictions*. He is the only American literary writer to be awarded the Order of the Aztec Eagle by the government of Mexico and he is prominently featured in the "Visitor's Key to Iceland."

WIND

Wind: what is it? You don't see it but you hear it, and you feel its force. It brings the rains, the drought, the cold, the heat, the locusts, the dust; it drives them away. It bangs the shutters, rustles the branches, flattens the house, spreads fire; it pushes the boats along or makes the waves that sink them. Its breezes in spring inspire affection, its howling in winter dread.

In China, the calendar was circular and divided into eight periods of forty-five days, each ruled by a wind coming from one of the eight directions, and each determining the rituals of government, the foods to be eaten, the robes worn, the punishment and pardon of criminals, the hours to wake or go to sleep, the times and places to take a walk, the gifts the Emperor should send.

There were "proper" winds and "evil" or "empty" winds: winds that blew from the right direction at the right time, and those that did not, causing sickness or chaos, for, it was said, the hundred diseases arose from the wind, and entered the 84,000 holes of the body, the acupuncture points, just as it blew through the hollows of the earth.

Everything is fine, says Chuang Tzu, when the world is still. "But when the wind blows, the ten thousand holes cry and moan. Haven't you heard them wailing on and on? In the awesome beauty of mountain forests, it's all huge trees a hundred feet around, and they're full of wailing hollows. . . When the wind's light, the harmony's gentle; but when the storm wails, it's a mighty chorus. And then, once the fierce wind has passed through, the holes are all empty again."

Wind was the vengeance of unhappy ancestors. Wind came from the mouths of snakes, and shamans wore snakes to blow them to the other world; in China or in Mexico, the shaman was portrayed in its gaping jaws. WIND, the character, was constructed from the pictograph of a sail and the pictograph of a snake. WIND plus SICKNESS meant "insane." WIND PURITY was sexual longing; HORSE WIND was a horse in heat; MALE WIND was sodomy. An anonymous woman in the 5th Century sings:

Spring flowers so delightful,
Spring birdsongs so moving,
Spring wind so passionate,
It blows open my silk skirt.

And WIND (*feng*) also meant "song." Song was how the government found out what the people were thinking, and the word came to mean "mood" or even "customs." The first Chinese anthology, the *Shi Ching*, the Book of Odes or Songs, opens with a section called *Kuo Feng*– STATE WIND– the songs, the moods, from the provincial states. The *Great Preface* to the *Shi Ching*, says: "By WIND superiors transform their inferiors, and by WIND inferiors satirize their superiors." It was said: "Hear the WIND [the songs from a certain state] and you will know the WIND [the mood of the people]."

WIND SCENE, a landscape. WIND LAND, wind and land, the local conditions. WIND WATER, wind and water, *fengshui*, the way one found one's place in the world. WIND RAIN, wind and rain, hardship. WIND WAVES, wind and waves, the changes in affairs. WIND TIDE, wind and tide, political unrest; the WIND GROUP, the opportunists.

The bird of paradise was the WIND BIRD; a WIND EXPRESSION an aristocratic demeanor; WIND GLORY, wind and glory, elegance and talent. WIND MOON, wind and moon, gaiety and a woman's seductive arts. WIND DUST, wind and dust, the difficulties of travel, military chaos, and the life of a prostitute.

A WIND MAN was a poet. WIND FLOW meant distinguished, sophisticated, talented in literature, and dissolute. WIND DELIGHT was merely humor, but WIND SORROW meant excellence in literature.

Hear the wind and you will know the wind. Wind blows, and the generations are its leaves. There was no higher praise than what was said of Confucius: He knows where the wind comes from.

ANECDOTAL EVIDENCE

1.

The *Huai Nan Tzu*, a Taoist book from the 2nd century B.C.E., tells the story of a man from ancient times, Kung Yu-ai, who for seven days was turned into a tiger. Fur grew over his body; his hands turned into claws; his teeth were those of a wild animal. His brother went to take a look; the tiger leapt and mauled him to death.

The tiger never knew he had once been a man. The man never knew he would someday be a tiger. The tiger was happy being a tiger, following his tiger nature. The man was happy being a man, following his human nature. Both enjoyed the happiness of being themselves, and neither suspected that they were equally happy as something entirely different.

2.

In the Midwest, a student told me how she lay awake at night, planning what she would wear the next day, including an alternative set of clothes in case there was a sudden change of weather. The most important element in her wardrobe was the socks. When wearing tennis shoes, the socks must match their color. However, when wearing leather shoes, the sock must match the blouse or sweater. The color of the pants or skirt served merely as a transition between socks and top.

These strictures, articulated at some length, went far beyond, or deeper than, fashion sense. In her childhood she had seen the Judy Garland movie *Meet Me in St. Louis* and had been impressed, not by the clang clang clang of the trolley, but by—she used the phrase—the *mise en scene*. All of the details of the furnishings and the clothes were historically accurate, and yet they had been color-coded to create a seamless, however unreal, world. The student felt that by similarly color-coding herself, she was transforming her own world and somehow entering into the perfection of that Technicolor Vicente Minnelli St. Louis. An outsider would have been unable to perceive the difference with any other student in a baggy white sweater, blue jeans, white socks, and black leather shoes, but those socks—that is, the whiteness of those socks—were the key to her happiness or a solace in her unhappiness.

3.

The *Lieh Tzu*, a Taoist book from the 3rd century C.E., tells the story of a man who couldn't find his axe, and suspected the boy next door of stealing it. For days he studied the boy, and from the boy's demeanor, his overly friendly way of saying good morning, his averted glance, and even his way of walking, it was obvious that the boy was the thief.

A few days later the man found his axe in the garden. The next time he saw the boy, there seemed to be nothing suspicious about him at all.

4.

On a cold, rainy, February night in New York, I remembered the story André Malraux used to tell—and which, at some remove, was told to me—about Mallarmé's cat, whose name, almost needless to say, was Blanche.

On a cold, rainy, February night in Paris, a thin and bedraggled alley cat, wandering the streets, looks in the window of Mallarmé's house and sees a white, fat, and fluffy cat dozing in an overstuffed chair by a blazing fire. He taps on the window:

"Comrade cat, how can you live in luxury and sleep so peacefully when your brothers are out here in the streets starving?"

"Have no fear, comrade," Blanche replied, "I'm only pretending to be Mallarmé's cat."

CHANGS

Chang Chih-ho, in the 8th century, lost his post under the Emperor and retreated to the mountains. He devoted himself to fishing, but never used any bait, for his object was not to catch fish.

Chang Tsai, in the 3rd century, was Secretary to the Heir Apparent. His ugliness was so extreme that children pelted him with stones whenever he went outside.

Chang Chio, in the 2nd century, called himself the Yellow God and led an army of 360,000 followers, all wearing yellow turbans. They brought down the Han Dynasty.

Chang Chao, one of the Five Men of Letters, fell off his horse in the 18th century, but impressed the Emperor by continuing to write poems with his left hand.

Chang Chen-chou, in the 8th century, was known for his unmatched honesty. Upon being appointed Governor of Shu-chou, he held a banquet for all his friends and relatives, gave them lavish gifts of silk and cash, and then, tears in his eyes, told them that from now on he could never see them again.

Chang Seng-yu, in the 6th century, painted a pair of dragons without eyes on the Temple of Peace and Joy, and warned that the painting should never be completed. A skeptic filled in the eyes, and the walls of the temple crashed to ruins as the dragons flew off.

Chang Chung, in the 14th century, was a philosopher who roamed the mountains wildly and always wore an iron cap.

Chang Ch'ien, in the 2nd century B.C.E., was the first Chinese to travel far to the west. He was captured in Bactria, and held prisoner for ten years before escaping to Fergana. From there he brought back the first walnuts and cultivated grapes, knotty bamboo and hemp, and the art of making wine.

This same Chang Ch'ien traveled so widely that it was believed he had found the source of the Yellow River, which flows down from the Milky Way: After following the river upstream for many months, he came to a city where he saw a young man leading an ox to water and a young woman spinning. He asked what place this was, and the girl gave him a shuttle and told him to show it to the noted astronomer Yen Chun-p'ing. Upon his return, the astronomer recognized the shuttle as belonging to the Spinning Damsel, the constellation Lyra, and said that he had noticed, at the exact moment Chang had entered the strange city, an errant star crossing between the Spinning Damsel and the Oxherding Boy.

Chang Ch'ao, in the 17th century, said: "Flowers must have butterflies, mountains must have streams, rocks must have moss, the ocean must have seaweed, old trees must have creepers, and people must have obsessions."

Chang Ch'ang, a scholar and governor in the 1st century B.C.E., was in the habit of personally painting his wife's eyebrows. When the Emperor asked him why, Chang replied that women consider eyebrows to be of the highest importance.

Both Chang Cho in the 8th century and Chang Chiu-ko in the 11th century could cut out paper butterflies that would flutter around and then return to their hands.

Chang Chu, a poet in the 13th century, wrote a line, "The cataclysm of red sheep," that no one has ever been able to explain.

Chang Hsu-ching, a Taoist, no one remembers exactly when, obtained the elixir of life and discovered that tigers would do his bidding.

Chang Jen-hsi, in the 18th century, wrote a treatise on ink.

Chang Li-hua, in the 6th century, was the Emperor's favorite concubine and renowned for the beauty of her hair, which was seven feet long.

Chang Jung, a poet in the 5th century, was given a fan made of white egret feathers by a Taoist priest, who told him that strange things should be given to strange people. The Emperor said that the kingdom couldn't stand to be without one man like Chang Jung and couldn't stand to be with two.

Chang Hsun held out bravely in the siege of Sui-yang in 756 and, as supplies and food ran short, even sacrificed his favorite concubine, to no avail. His patriotic rage caused him to grind his teeth with such fury that after his execution it was discovered that he had no teeth left at all.

Chang Fang-p'ing, in the 11th century, was a prolific writer who never wrote a rough draft.

The family of Chang Kung-i, in the 7th century, was noted for having had nine generations of harmonious living. When the Emperor asked how this was possible, he called for pen and paper, and wrote the character "patience" over and over.

Chang Kuo was one of the Eight Immortals of the 8th century. The Empress sent a messenger to summon him to court, but by the time the messenger arrived Chang was already dead. Later he appeared again, and the Empress sent another messenger who fell into a swoon that lasted for years. A third messenger was successful, and Chang entertained the Court by becoming invisible and drinking poison, but he refused to have his portrait placed in the Hall of Worthies.

Chang I, in the 2nd century, wrote an encyclopedia of miscellaneous information. Chang K'ai, in the same century, could raise fogs.

Chang Ying, in the 17th century, was the official Reader to the Emperor.

Chang Tsu, in the 7th century, was too critical and always getting into trouble, but it was said that his essays were like a thousand pieces of gold chosen from a thousand pieces of gold. This meant that they were all precious.

Chang Ying-wen, in the 16th century, could never pass the examinations, as he thought only about antiques. Fortunately he became a connoisseur.

When Chang Shao died, sometime in the Han Dynasty, he appeared to his best friend Fan Shih in a dream. Fan immediately set out for the funeral, many provinces away. For weeks no one was able to lift Chang's coffin, until Fan rode up on a white horse, dressed in mourning.

Chang Huang-yen, the last supporter of the Ming Dynasty in the 17th century, retreated to a barren island, where he trained apes to warn him of an enemy approach.

Chang Tsao, in the 9th century, would paint trees simultaneously using his finger and a worn stump of a brush—one for the living matter, the other for the dead branches and fallen leaves.

Chang Hua, in the 3rd century, wrote a famous rhapsody or rhymed prose poem (*fu*) on the wren: The wren is a tiny bird. It eats only a few grains; it makes its nest on a single branch; it can only fly a few feet; it takes up little space and does no harm. Its feathers are drab; it is useless to humankind; but it too receives the force of life. Ducks and geese can fly up to the clouds, yet they are shot down with arrows, for their flesh is plump. Kingfishers and peacocks must die because their feathers are beautiful. The falcon is fierce, but is kept on a tether; the parrot is intelligent, but is locked in a cage, where it is forced to repeat its master's words. Only the little wren, worthless and unlovely, is free.

Chang Hua, like many poets, did not listen to himself. He came from a respected family that had fallen into poverty. In his youth he was a goatherd, but his intelligence was so notable that he somehow managed to marry the daughter of a prominent official and was appointed as an erudite to the Ministry of Ceremonies. From there he became Deputy Compiler, then a Gentleman of Palace Writers, and the Emperor often consulted him on matters of ritual and protocol. In 267 he was given the title of Marquis of the Passes, and in 270 invented a system of organizing and cataloging the Imperial Library that was used for centuries. He went on to become the Marquis of Guangwu and the Military Governor of Yuchou. In 287, the ridgepole in the Great Hall of the Imperial Ancestral Temple collapsed and Chang, now Director of the Ministry of Ceremonies, was held responsible and fell in disgrace. A few years later, with the accession of a new Emperor, Chang returned to the Court, and held posts as Imperial Household Grandee of the Right, Overseer of the Masters of Writing, Duke of Chuangwu and, his highest post, Minister of Works. In 299, he was caught in palace intrigues and refused to join what became a successful coup d'etat. He and all his sons and their sons were executed.

PHILIP WHALEN

BORN IN 1923 in Portland, Oregon, Philip Whalen grew up in The Dalles, a small town situated where the Columbia River narrows into a thunderous gorge. He served in the U.S. Army Air Corps during World War II. A fellow aviator turned him on to the writings of Gertrude Stein, shifting him away from his ambition to write novels like Thomas Wolfe's. Returning to Portland he attended Reed College, eventually rooming with Gary Snyder and Lew Welch, and finding the haiku studies by R.H. Blyth which led him to Zen. He moved to San Francisco, taking part in the historic Six Gallery reading with Allen Ginsberg, Gary Snyder, and Michael McClure. A timely grant led to a residency in Kyoto, Japan, captured in his heartbreakingly funny wise poem, *Scenes of Life at the Capital.* His innovative poetry—less popularized than work by close friends Allen Ginsberg and Jack Kerouac—has exerted a probably deeper influence on innovative younger poets, including Leslie Scalapino and Tyler Doherty who appear in this anthology. In fact Philip's 1967 collection *On Bear's Head* was a significant "underground" influence, sending dozens of younger writers into poetry that is "a picture or graph of a mind moving." Philip moved into the San Francisco Zen Center in 1972 and the following year was ordained Zen Buddhist monk *(unsui).* In 1991 he became abbot at the Hartford Street Zen Center, just off San Francisco's Castro Street, taking the lion throne with the words, "The seat is empty. No one sits in it. Please take good care of yourselves." *Overtime: Selected Poems* appeared in 1999, collecting work from a dozen books. The only contributor to the present anthology no longer alive, Philip Zenshin Whalen died in 2001.

THE SIMPLE LIFE

I say "I love" and that's enough
The elephant can guess
I'm infatuated with her
If I feed her a peanut and speak gentle nothings
She'll remember me kindly, perhaps
No embarrassment on either side.

No proof, no justification
Get on with it
        since I can't get along without it
        (some kind of torment?)

Dull smokey agates at Stinson Beach
    whether I love you or not
Only another idea
Maybe nobody loves you or me
        Pellegrini & Cudahy

23-24 VI 77

SOMEWHERE ELSE

What is not there that one is missing
What is the pitted viper hissing
          "Health & money. Rice & beans"
     Kiss me quick

Now everything is completed, quite
Suddenly. The supper is washed & set away
But this music is called "Dinner Jazz"
I call myself no body replies.
The high pressure ridge has broke. Tremendous
Winds crash in. The piano turns to stone.

"I cannot hear of it without tears. {R.I.P}"

"What a sensitive darling you are!"

27 1 81

THE ELIZABETHAN PHRASE

"... so the world runs on wheels," they used to say
One of which, I think, has a flat side
Thus accounting for such anomalies as these
Yellow avalanche lilies blooming in
And through the snowfield on Sourdough Mountain
Their color burns the ice away
Big floppy tulip leaves   the ears of deer
Deer lilies probably poison to any other belly.

25 VIII 82

FOR SHUNKO ENJO

Don't
Slobber on the paper. And then it was

Lunch time. Let us eat sandwiches:
A solo for flugelhorn.
Abysmal Dante, rise again!
The stream flows between rocks or over them.
Natural History doesn't hold the answer.
Molecular theory of recombinative R N A and

Didn't I tell you Not
to dribble on the paper?
Now it will all commence to
dissociate. Can I say that.
Why don't you dry your fingers
after they have been playing in the water,

It is impatience fleeing from Incapacity, as
W^M Blake might have said, or the towel didn't perform its proper nature, its little fibres being
clogged with silt, soap, tiny flakes of dead skin—
the towel must be restored by the laundry.
T I G E R B A L M   G A R D E N
Tromba marina

23 I 83

DHARMAKAYA

The real thing is always an imitation
Consider new plum blossoms behind the zendō

20 I 81

PATHOGENESIS

" . . . out where the West begins . . ."

{Scranton?}

{virgin birth?}

is "the beginning of suffering"
which ends temporarily at death

29 or 30 vi 86

EPIGRAMS & IMITATIONS

I
ACTIONS OF BUDDHA

Clip cuticle; drink orange juice
"be confirmed by 10,000 things"
(the next line after that is delinquent)
turtles

II
UPON THE POET'S PHOTOGRAPH

This printed face doesn't see
A curious looking in;
Big map of nothing.

III
FROM THE JAPANESE OF KAKINOMOTO HITOMARO

What though my shorts are threadbare
I deserve all your love

IV
FALSE SENRYŪ

A cough
waits for the bus.

V
PERPETUUM MOBILE

Everybody has a car
But something's wrong with it

GRIEVANCES

Tears & recriminations don't cut no ice
Constantly the Northern Star bewilders the astrolabe
You can't get a fix on what's constantly moving
Not without instant electronics, can you.
Oh, and if, and if, and if, and if, and if!

BOULDER 21 VII 87

THE IMPERFECT SONNET

"The person of whom you speak is dead"
Where is the better crystal?
One came in last night & took it; this one
Held the papers on the table
Now I want topaze.

In the middle of the night—
The glass doors locked, nothing else missing
Worthless Quartz eccentrically shaped gone
As Emperor Nicholas Romanov
As "Bebe" Rebozo

Say that you love me say
That you will bring me
A delicious cup of coffee
A topaze cup! From Silesia—
Property of Hapsburg Emperors
The better crystal is upstairs.

NEW SMYRNA BEACH 12 XI 88

ON THE WAY TO THE ZENDŌ

A reverse wind blows freeway sounds up-canyon
    through yellow leaves
Ducks quack and cluck flying to Bosque del Apache
SOME VERSIONS OF THE PASTORAL whistle in one ear,
    out the other.
Christopher Robin, Pooh, and Piglet
Stomping through the Hundred Acre wood.

18 IX 86

HYMNUS AD PATREM SINENSIS

I praise those ancient Chinamen
Who left me a few words,
Usually a pointless joke or a silly question
A line of poetry drunkenly scrawled on the margin of a quick
                splashed picture—bug, leaf,
                caricature of Teacher
        on paper held together now by little more than ink
        & their own strength brushed momentarily over it

Their world & several others since
Gone to hell in a handbasket, they knew it—
Cheered as it whizzed by—
& conked out among the busted spring rain cherryblossom winejars
Happy to have saved us all.

31 VIII 58

PERMISSIONS

Will Alexander: "Asia" from *Asia & Haiti* (Sun & Moon Press). Copyright © 1995 by Will Alexander. Reprinted by permission of the author.

Tsering Wangmo Dhompa: "Sun Storm," "How Thubten Sang His Songs," "Bardo," and "Body as What is Remembered" from *Rules of the House* (Apogee Press). Copyright © 2002 by Tsering Wangmo Dhompa. Reprinted by permission of author.

Tyler Doherty: "Bodhidharma Never Came to Hatboro" from *Bodhidharma Never Came to Hatboro* (Bootstrap Productions). Copyright © 2004 by Tyler Doherty. Reprinted by permission of Bootstrap Productions.

Lawrence Ferlinghetti: "A Buddha In The Woodpile" from *These Are My Rivers*, copyright © 1993 by Lawrence Ferlinghetti. Reprinted by permission of New Directions Publishing Corp.

Norman Fischer: *Success* (Singing Horse Press), copyright © 2000 by Norman Fischer. Reprinted by permission of the author.

Jane Hirshfield: "Against Certainty" and "Why Bodhidharma Went to Howard Johnson's," copyright © 2002 by Jane Hirshfield. "Lighthouse," copyright © 2003 by Jane Hirshfield. "Theology," "The Dead Do Not Want Us Dead," and "After Long Silence," copyright © 2001 by Jane Hirshfield. Reprinted by permission of the author. "Reading Chinese Poetry Before Dawn" and "Studying Wu Wei, Muir Beach" from *The Lives of the Heart* by Jane Hirshfield, copyright © 1997 by Jane Hirshfield. Reprinted by permission of HarperCollins Publishers Inc. "Inspiration" from *The October*

Palace by Jane Hirshfield, copyright © 1994 by Jane Hirshfield. Reprinted by permission of HarperCollins Publishers Inc. "Recalling a Sung Dynasty Landscape" from *Of Gravity & Angles;* Wesleyan Poetry Series; Wesleyan University Press distributed by University Press of New England; copyright © 1988 by Jane Hirshfield. Reprinted by permission of Wesleyan University Press. "A Cedary Fragrance" from *Given Sugar, Given Salt* by Jane Hirshfield, copyright © 2001 by Jane Hirshfield. Reprinted by permission of HarperCollins Publishers Inc.

Lawson Fusao Inada: "A High-Five for I-5 and "Picking Up Stones" from *Drawing the Line.* Copyright © 1997 by Lawson Fusao Inada. Reprinted by permission of Coffee House Press, Minneapolis, Minnesota.

Joanne Kyger: All poems from *Again* (La Alameda Press). Copyright © 2001 by Joanne Kyger. Reprinted by permission of La Alameda Press, Albuquerque, New Mexico.

Michael McClure: "Plum Stones," "Thoreau's Eyes," and "Unchanged" from *Plum Stones: Cartoons of No Heaven* (O Books). Copyright © 2002 by Michael McClure. Reprinted by permission of the author. "Touching the Edge" and "Haiku Rows" from *Touching the Edge: Dharma Devotions from the Hummingbird Sangha,* by Michael McClure © 1999. Reprinted by arrangement with Shambhala Publications, Inc., Boston, www.shambhala.com.

Harryette Mullen: "Souvenir from Anywhere," "Mantra for a Classless Society, Or Mr. Roget's Neighborhood," "Zen Acorn," "Xenophobic Nightmare in a Foreign Language," and "Kamasutra Sutra" from *Sleeping with the Dictionary* (University of California Press). Copyright © 2002 by Harryette Mullen. Reprinted by permission of the author.

Hoa Nguyen: Poems from *Your Ancient See Through* (Subpress). Copyright © 2002 by Hoa Nguyen. Reprinted by permission of the author.

Shin Yu Pai: All poems from *Equivalence* (La Alameda Press). Copyright © 2003 by Shin Yu Pai. Reprinted by permission of La Alameda Press, Albuquerque, New Mexico.

Miriam Sagan: "Contentment" from *True Body* (Parallax Press). Copyright © 1991. Reprinted by permission of Parallax Press. "Mountain Peak Grave" from *The Widow's Coat* (Ahsahta Press). Copyright © 1999 by Miriam Sagan. Reprinted by permission of the author. "Prayer Flag" and "Reading Chiyo-Ni, 1703–1775, Japanese Woman Haikuist" from *Future Tense of Ash* (Lilliput / Modest Proposal Chapbook). Copyright © 2002. Reprinted by permission of the author. "South Ridge Zendo" from *Aegean Doorway* (Zephyr Press). Copyright © 1984 by Miriam Sagan. Reprinted by permission of Zephyr Press.

Leslie Scalapino: From *It's go in quiet illumined grassland* (The Post-Apollo Press). Copyright © 2002 by Leslie Scalapino. Reprinted by the permission of The Post-Apollo Press, Sausalito, CA.

Andrew Schelling: "Haibun," and "Tyger Tyger" from *Tea Shack Interior: New & Selected Poetry* (Talisman House Publishers). Copyright © 2002 by Andrew Schelling. Reprinted by permission of Talisman House Publishers, Jersey City, New Jersey.

Gary Snyder: "Working on the '58 Willys Pickup," "Breasts," and "Walking Through Myoshin-ji" from *Axe Handles.* Copyright © 1983 by Gary Snyder. Reprinted by permission of the author and Shoemaker & Hoard, Publishers, Washington, D.C. "For Carole," "Really the Real," "Waiting for a Ride," "Coffee, Markets, Blossoms," and "No Shadow" from *Danger on Peaks.* Copyright © 2004 by Gary Snyder. Reprinted by permission of the author and Shoemaker & Hoard, Publishers, Washington, D.C.

Nathaniel Tarn: "Hearing About the Virtual Destruction of Pain," "The First Zen Abbess of America," "Retreat Toward the Spring," "A Man whose Name Rhymes with Peace," "As If There were any Matter," and "The Heart Stumbles in Darkness" from *Seeing America First* (Coffee House Press). Copyright © 1989 by Nathaniel Tarn. Reprinted by permission of Coffee House Press, Minneapolis, Minnesota.

Chase Twichell: All poems from the forthcoming *Dog Language* to be published by Copper Canyon Press, 2005. Copyright © 2005 by Chase Twichell. Reprinted by permission of Copper Canyon Press, Port Townsend, WA.

Cecilia Vicuña: "The Shadow of a Loom" from *Shamballa.* Reprinted by permission of the author. "Untitled" from *Unravelling Words and the Weaving of Water* (Graywolf Press). Copyright © 1992 by Cecilia Vicuña. Reprinted by permission of the author. "With A Little Notebook At The Met" reprinted from *Sibila #1,* Revista de Poesia e Cultura, Brazil, copyright © 2001. Reprinted by permission of the author. "fables of the beginning and remains of the origin" from *Instan* (Kelsey St. Press). Copyright © 2002 by Cecilia Vicuña. Reprinted by permission of Kelsey St. Press.

Philip Whalen: Poems reprinted from *Some of These Days* (Desert Rose), copyright © 1999 by Philip Whalen, and *Overtime* (Penguin Books), copyright © 1999 by Philip Whalen. Reprinted by permission of the Estate of Philip Whalen.

FURTHER READING

I AM LISTING ANTHOLOGIES of North American Buddhist poetry that have previously appeared. Additionally I thought it useful to provide a list of good available translations of poetry from Buddhist Asia, particularly India, China, Japan, and Tibet. Including all such translations into English would amount to hundreds of pages, so this is a selection of influential and currently available titles, with an emphasis on those done by contributors to the present collection. Because a number of poets in this anthology have written about Buddhist practice and how it influences their poetry, I have also listed books containing their essays, interviews, journals, memoirs, & so forth, that have been particularly significant.

—A.S.

ANTHOLOGIES OF NORTH AMERICAN BUDDHIST POETRY

Gach, Gary, ed. *What Book!? Buddha Poems from Beat to Hiphop.* Berkeley: Parallax Press, 1998. Freewheeling and fun; contains numerous poems, calligraphy, and chopped-up Dharma talks from dozens of poets, Buddhist teachers, musicians, and artists, arranged according to topics. Good biographical notes on the range of contributors.

Johnson, Kent and Craig Paulenich, eds. *Beneath a Single Moon: Buddhism in Contemporary American Poetry.* Boston: Shambhala Publications, 1991. The first serious and substantial collection of American poets influenced by Buddhism. Most of the forty-four poets contribute statements or essays on the relation of Buddhist practice to poetry. Introduction by Gary Snyder.

Smith, Larry and Ray MacNeice, ed. *America Zen: A Gathering of Poets.* Huron, Ohio: Bottom Dog Press, 2004. Specifically focused on Zen, a range of poets not often found together in journals or anthologies. Each poet is represented by several pages of poetry and a 300-word statement on Zen practice.

Tonkinson, Carole. *Big Sky Mind: Buddhism and the Beat Generation.* New York: Riverhead Books, 1995. Focuses on the first high-profile generation of poets who embraced Buddhism, the Beats. Kerouac, Snyder, Ginsberg, and others. This anthology was collected under the aegis of *Tricycle: The Buddhist Journal,* where Carole Tonkinson served as one of the early editors.

TRANSLATIONS OF BUDDHIST POETRY FROM ASIA

Barnstone, Tony and Chou Ping. *The Art of Writing: Teachings of the Chinese Masters.* Boston: Shambhala Publications, 1996. Gathers in lively translation three of the major early Chinese pieces on poetic composition, including Lu Ji's renowned "The Art of Writing." A final section, "Stories and Aphorisms about Literature" picks and chooses pithy extracts from various Chinese sources.

Berg, Steven. *Crow with no Mouth: Ikkyu, 15th Century Zen Master.* Port Townsend: Copper Canyon, 1989. Colloquial versions by one of the founders of *American Poetry Review.* Ikkyu, a unique figure in Zen for his celebration of sexual love, was also known as Crazy Cloud. Unorthodox, bawdy, contemptuous of "fame-and-fortune Zen," his poems celebrate what Ikkyu termed his "whorehouse joy."

Blyth, R. H. *Haiku.* 4 vols. Tokyo: Hokuseido Press, 1949–52. The first significant volumes of haiku to make their way into the hands of Western readers. Still in print today, they are full of Japan's best haiku (in translation), embedded in commentary that often points out the Zen instinct behind the poems. Each volume contains poems for a single season: spring, summer, autumn, and winter.

Blyth, Reginald H. *History of Haiku.* 2 vols. Tokyo: Hokuseido Press, 1963–64. Though a bit dated, these volumes give a fine overview of the poets, their shifting styles and practices, and the Zen impulse behind haiku. Deservedly still in print.

Bynner, Witter and Kiang Kang-hu. *The Jade Mountain: A Chinese Anthology.* New York: Alfred A. Knopf, 1931. After Ezra Pound, Bynner was the next American poet to publish substantial amounts of Chinese poetry in translation. The anthology contains some of the most moving translations done, and should be more widely read. It was Bynner who convinced Kenneth Rexroth to turn his attentions to Chinese classical poetry.

Corman, Cid and Kamaike Susumu. *Back Roads to Far Towns: Basho's Oku-no-Hosomichi.* New York: Mushinsha / Grossman, 1968. Corman's translation is perhaps the quirkiest one available of Basho's best-known work. It may also be the one that best conveys the density, complexity, and craft of the original. Corman lived most of his adult life in Japan, was a prolific poet and translator, and was the first publisher of Gary Snyder's *Riprap.*

de Cristofor, Violet Kazue. *May Sky: There is Always Tomorrow. An Anthology of Japanese American Concentration Camp Kaiko Haiku.* Los Angeles: Sun & Moon Press, 1997. Account of the free-style haiku *kai* (clubs or societies) that existed among Japanese-Americans in the decades before the bombing of Pearl Harbor. After all citizens of Japanese ancestry were removed from the West Coast—most to detention centers or concentration camps inland—the haiku clubs formed again. This book shows the extent to which haiku was being written in North America by immigrant Japanese citizens, well before English-speaking American poets popularized the form.

Fields, Rick and Brian Cutillo. *The Turquoise Bee: The Love Songs of the Sixth Dalai Lama.* New York: HarperCollins, 1998. Good translations of these brief, explicitly sexual love poems, which stand alone in Tibetan literature. The Sixth Dalai Lama must have been studied in classical Sanskrit poetry—many of his erotic themes are modeled on India's poetry, transplanted to the Tibetan plateau.

Hamill, Sam. *The Essential Basho.* Boston: Shambhala Publications, 1999. Fine contemporary translations. Includes the main poetic journals of Basho and a great deal of his haiku. Also see Hamill's other translations from the Chinese and Japanese, including selections of Li Po and Tu Fu, and an edition of the *Chuang Tzu.* Hamill, like his early mentor Kenneth Rexroth, has put translation of Asian poetry at the core of his own substantial original work.

Hass, Robert. *The Essential Haiku: Versions of Basho, Buson, & Issa.* Hopewell, New Jersey: Ecco Press, 1994. A particularly good overview of Japan's three most influential haiku poets. Hass's introduction and essays flesh out the archaic roots of haiku, and the Buddhist principles underlying the approach to Japanese poetry. Includes a fine selection of sayings and aphorisms by Basho on the Way of Poetry.

Hinton, David. *The Selected Poems of Li Po.* New York: New Directions, 1996. A solid selection of Li Po's poetry. Li Po considered himself a Taoist immortal exiled to earth. He was a dear friend of Tu Fu and a wildly imaginative and romantic poet. Legend says he drowned trying to embrace the moon's image in a pond after a night of drinking.

Hinton, David. *The Selected Poems of T'ao Ch'ien.* Port Townsend: Copper Canyon, 1993. Hinton is a prolific translator of Chinese poetry and has retranslated the Four Classics for our era. His Tao Ch'ien brings alive the poet whose tone was likened to "gnawing on withered wood"—and who established the stance of so many Chinese poets afterward, living as a recluse far from the turbulence of the State, and making frequent visits to the halls of Ch'an Buddhist temples.

Hinton, David. *The Selected Poems of Tu Fu.* New York: New Directions, 1989. Fine renditions of China's most renowned poet, Tu Fu, who is considered a buddha of poetry.

Hirshfield, Jane and Mariko Aratani. *The Ink Dark Moon: Love Poems by Ono no Komachi and Izumi Shikibu, Women of the Ancient Court of Japan.* Riverside, New Jersey: Random House, 1990. Excellent translations of two mysterious, tragic poets. Komachi's legacy of poems gave birth to numerous legends, and she was a frequent subject of Noh plays, her ghost again and again returning to the old scenes of her love affairs.

LaFleur, William R. *Awesome Nightfall: The Life, Times, and Poetry of Saigyo.* Boston: Wisdom Publications, 2003. Saigyo was a twelfth-century wandering Buddhist priest and poet. Along with Basho he established the model of the Japanese writer who is on perpetual pilgrimage in search of the sources of poetry, and whose pursuit of poems is a Buddhist discipline. LaFleur's book includes a full account of Saigyo's complex life and mind.

Milarepa. *Tibet's Great Yogi Milarepa: A Biography from the Tibetan.* Edited with introduction and annotations by W. Y. Evans-Wentz. London: Oxford University Press, 1951. The first translation into English of Tibet's best-known poet, who after a violent, murderous youth, devoted himself to enlightenment and left long instructional songs that are still chanted ceremonially by Tibetan monks and nuns in exile.

Miner, Earl. *Japanese Poetic Diaries.* Berkeley: University of California Press, 1969. Fine study and readable translations of important poetic journals, including Izumi Shikabu, Basho, and others.

Murcott, Susan. *The First Buddhist Women.* Berkeley: Parallax Press, 1991. A study with translations of the *Therigatha,* the collection of poems by women who were direct disciples of Shakyamuni Buddha.

O'Connor, Mike. *When I Find You Again It Will Be in Mountains: Selected Poems of Chia Tao*. Boston: Wisdom Publications, 2000. The first—and very good—collection in English of this T'ang Dynasty Buddhist poet, previously known to Americans through only a couple of famous poems. (Alan Watts's *Cloud Hidden, Whereabouts Unknown* took its title from a Chia Tao poem.) Chia Tao followed the way of voluntary poverty in order to pursue poetry, and at his death is said to have left only a zither and a sick donkey behind.

Pine, Red. *The Collected Songs of Cold Mountain.* Revised and expanded. Port Townsend: Copper Canyon, 2000. Red Pine knows more of Buddhist and

Taoist China first-hand than any other American. His excellent translations are backed by good scholarship, a resilient and explicitly anti-academic stance, and direct contact with the people, landscapes, and monuments of China.

Pine, Red. *Poems of the Masters: China's Classic Anthology of T'ang and Sung Dynasty Verse.* Port Townsend: Copper Canyon, 2003. Excellent translations, with Red Pine's mini-essays on each poem, which discuss the poet, the times, and the circumstances that brought the poem into existence. This was China's own textbook of verse until banned during the Cultural Revolution.

Pine, Red and Mike O'Connor, eds. *The Clouds Should Know Me By Now: Buddhist Poet Monks of China.* Boston: Wisdom Publications, 1994. Excellent account of the lengthy tradition of Buddhist monks who left tracks of their lives in poetry—six poets presented by six different American scholar-translators. Introduction by Andrew Schelling.

Pound, Ezra. *The Translations of Ezra Pound.* New York: New Directions, 1963. Includes the ground-breaking poems of *Cathay* and Pound's versions of the Noh theater, both drawn from the notebooks of Boston art critic and Buddhist, Ernest Fenollosa.

Pound, Ezra and Ernest Fenollosa. *The Chinese Written Character as a Medium for Poetry.* San Francisco: City Lights, 1968. One of the most significant manifestos of the Modernist period for poetry, this essay has influenced nearly every American poet's view of the Chinese language and China's classical poetry.

Pound, Ezra and Ernest Fenollosa. *Noh: The Classic Noh Theater of Japan.* New York: New Directions, 1959. These plays, underpinned by Buddhist metaphysics and folklore, are magical, exquisitely formal, and are performed with aristocratic restraint. Pound's versions are far and away the best. They influenced William Butler Yeats's approach to the theater. Kenneth Rexroth thought one of Pound's Noh versions, "Nishikigi," the best American poem of the twentieth century, and Charles Olson held "Hagoromo" in similar regard.

Rexroth, Kenneth. *One Hundred Poems from the Chinese.* New York: New Directions, 1956. The influence of Rexroth's translations can't be overstated. This was his first volume of poems from the Orient, and includes large selections of Tu Fu (who became Rexroth's own model for verse) and Su Tung-p'o. See also Rexroth's many other collections of both Chinese and Japanese poetry, including the volumes *Women Poets of China* and *Women Poets of Japan.*

Rhys Davids, Caroline A.F. *Psalms of the Early Buddhists.* London: The Pali Text Society, 1909. Rather dated and stuffy translations, but the one place you can find both books of early Indian Buddhist poetry, the *Theragatha* and the *Therigatha,* translated in full.

Rothenberg, Jerome, ed. *Technicians of the Sacred: A Range of Poetries from Africa, America, Asia, Europe & Oceania.* Second edition, revised and enlarged. Berkeley: University of California Press, 1985. An inspired anthology of poetry from across the planet, and one of the most influential books on American poetry from the 1960s onward. Rothenberg's lively commentaries link traditional practices of tribal and non-Western poets to contemporary writers in America. Should be on everyone's bookshelf.

Schelling, Andrew. *The Cane Groves of Narmada River: Erotic Poems from Old India.* San Francisco: City Lights, 1997. A selection of poetry written in classical Sanskrit during the peak of Buddhism in India. The poems are largely secular, but have a complex spiritual philosophy behind them. They show the cosmopolitan, open-minded aspect of India's great civilization at the period when Mahayana Buddhism and tantric Hinduism were coming to full expression. See also *Erotic Love Poems from India: A Translation of the Amarushataka.* Boston: Shambhala Publications, 2004.

Schelling, Andrew and Anne Waldman. *Songs of the Sons & Daughters of Buddha.* Boston: Shambhala Publications, 1996. Selections from the *Therigatha* and *Theragatha*—poems by the early wandering disciples of Buddha. These versions work to restore the exhilaration of performance to the oral poetry. The poems here once served the early sangha as goads to practice.

Snyder, Gary. *Riprap & Cold Mountain Poems.* San Francisco: North Point Press, 1990. Includes Snyder's crisp, informed, colloquial translations of twenty-four poems of the T'ang Dynasty recluse Han Shan, or Cold Mountain. These versions have had an enormous influence on American Buddhist approaches to voluntary poverty, mountain adventure, and straight-talking poetry.

Stevens, John. *Wild Ways: Zen Poems of Ikkyu.* Buffalo, New York: White Pine Press, 2003. Good translations of the Crazy Cloud Zen poet.

Sze, Arthur. *The Silk Dragon: Translations from the Chinese.* Port Townsend: Copper Canyon, 2001. A range of excellent translations, mostly classical poetry with a few twentieth-century pieces to round out the book. Includes an insightful introduction on Sze's method of getting the far-off language into American poetry.

Watson, Burton. *Four Huts: Asian Writings on the Simple Life.* Boston: Shambhala Publications, 1994. Translations of four separate Chinese and Japanese poets including Basho, each of whom wrote an account of a retreat in a modest hut.

Watson, Burton. *Ryokan: Zen Monk-Poet of Japan.* New York: Columbia University Press, 1977. Excellent translations of this wandering poet-monk of Japan.

Watson, Burton. *Su Tung-p'o: Selections from a Sung Dynasty Poet.* New York: Columbia University Press, 1965. Fine translations of the Ch'an Buddhist adept Su Tung-p'o—one of China's greatest poets—by a superb scholar-translator. The book was originally dedicated to Watson's friends Gary Snyder and Joanne Kyger.

Weinberger, Eliot. *The New Directions Anthology of Classical Chinese Poetry.* New York: New Directions, 2003. Translations by Ezra Pound, William Carlos Williams, Kenneth Rexroth, Gary Snyder, and David Hinton. The one book to own if you don't have the money or the space to own all the separate collections of Chinese poetry translated by these five excellent poets. Weinberger's introduction is superb.

Weinberger, Eliot and Octavio Paz. *Nineteen Ways of Looking at Wang Wei.* Mt. Kisko, New York: Moyer Bell, 1987. One of the closest looks at a single poem ever published—the poem being "Deer Park" by the Buddhist painter, poet, and calligraphy master Wang Wei. Translations by many Western writers, with each scrutinized for its assumptions, and for what the translator has missed or added in. Weinberger's comments are point-on—and enormously funny as well.

PROSE: ESSAYS, JOURNALS, INTERVIEWS

Aitken, Robert. *A Zen Wave: Basho's Haiku and Zen.* Washington D.C.: Shoemaker & Hoard, 2003. Zen talks, each beginning with a close look at one of Basho's haiku. Aitken, a Zen roshi and founder of the Diamond Sangha in Honolulu, met R.H. Blyth in an internment camp in Japan during World War II, and has devoted his life to Buddhist study. He is an excellent speaker and writer.

Cage, John. *For the Birds: John Cage in Conversation with Daniel Charles.* Boston: Marion Boyars, 1981. Many anecdotes of Cage's use of Hindu aesthetic theories, Zen Buddhist studies with D.T. Suzuki, and *I Ching* methods to compose literary texts and music. All of Cage's writings are important additions to American Zen, and everyone should know his book *Silence.* Cage continually tried to find questions not answers, crafting his own life like a sequence of koans.

Fields, Rick. *How the Swans Came to the Lake: A Narrative History of Buddhism in America.* Boston: Shambhala Publications, 1981. Delightfully readable account of Buddhism's first decades in North America, with anecdotes and interviews of the teachers, poets, writers, and thinkers who helped get things going.

Fischer, Norman. *The Narrow Roads of Japan.* San Francisco: Ex Nihilo Press, 1998. Account by this Zen priest and experimental poet of his travels through Japan. The title is an echo of Basho's best-known prose/verse diary, and this book keeps to the earlier poet's instinct.

Friedlander, Benjamin and Andrew Schelling, eds. *Jimmy & Lucy's House of "K,"* issue 9, 1990, "The Poetics of Emptiness." Contains transcripts of the 1987 gathering at Green Gulch Farms Zen Center, hosted by Norman Fischer and titled "The Poetics of Emptiness." Talks and poems by Gary Snyder, Philip Whalen, Jane Hirshfield, and many others. Hard to find, but may be available in a few libraries.

Ginsberg, Allen. *Indian Journals.* San Francisco: Dave Haselwood Books / City Lights, 1970. Covers the year in which Ginsberg lived and traveled in India with his companion Peter Orlovsky. Many of the poet's famous India poems appear first in these pages, and there are gripping accounts of tantric practices on the burning ghats of Calcutta. Also see the collections of poetry, interviews, essays, and other journals by Ginsberg, most of which remain in print.

Hamill, Sam. *Basho's Ghost.* Seattle: Broken Moon Press, 1989. Excellent gathering of essays, all focused on a Buddhist approach to poetry. Hamill is deeply schooled in the world's poetry tradition and can speak with tough, straightforward elegance on ancient and contemporary writings.

Hirshfield, Jane. *Nine Gates: Entering the Mind of Poetry.* New York: HarperCollins, 1997. An indispensable book for its efforts to understand the practice of poetry from a Buddhist point of view. Hirshfield is equally at home in Eastern or Western literary halls.

Kerouac, Jack. *The Dharma Bums.* New York: Viking Press, 1958. The book that made Dharma revolutionaries the most up-to-date people around. It calls for a rucksack revolution, the model or hero a poet-mountaineer, Japhy Ryder, modeled on Kerouac's friend Gary Snyder. This novel may be the original text of a distinctly American form of Buddhism.

Kerouac, Jack. *Some of the Dharma.* New York: Penguin, 1997. The huge manuscript of poems, notes, haiku, and inspired Buddhist writing, painstakingly compiled for decades and left unpublished in Kerouac's lifetime. A volume you can wander in for months.

Kyger, Joanne. *Strange Big Moon: The Japan and India Journals* 1960–1964. Berkeley: North Atlantic Books, 2000. Covers the years in Kyoto that Kyger belonged to an expatriate circle of American writers, studying Zen and

Japanese culture. Includes account of a trip through India with Gary Snyder, joined much of the time by Ginsberg and Orlovsky. Visits to the Dalai Lama, Lama Govinda, and other notable figures. Carries the dry, funny, unsentimental tone that is a hallmark of Kyger's poetry.

McClure, Michael. *Lighting the Corners: On Art, Nature, and the Visionary: Essays & Interviews.* Albuquerque: University of New Mexico Press, 1993. The best candid collection of talks, conversations, and occasional pieces by McClure, with much history, personal anecdote, and insight into the impact of spiritual and visionary poets.

McClure, Michael. *Scratching the Beat Surface.* San Francisco: North Point Press, 1982. The first account of Beat literature written by a participating poet. Many good anecdotes and much insight into the writings.

Meltzer, David, ed. *San Francisco Beat: Talking with the Poets.* San Francisco: City Lights, 2001. Expanded edition of a long out-of-print seminal document. This edition has interviews with di Prima, McClure, Kyger, Snyder, Whalen, Ferlinghetti, Rexroth, and other San Francisco-based poets: conversations range across poetry, Zen, anarchism, globalism, the Kabbalah, and the Internet.

Pendell, Dale. *Pharmako/Poiea.* San Francisco: Mercury House, 1996. See also volume 2, *Pharmako/Dynamis*, 2002. Pendell's explorations of the effect of "stimulating plants, potions & herbcraft" on human consciousness go deep into alchemy, Zen, anthropology, and biochemistry. These books are full of "dangerous knowledge," which Gary Snyder observes to be an antidote to "even more dangerous ignorance." The playfulness, good humor, and edge of danger give a Zen-inflected balance to this remarkable project.

Rexroth, Kenneth. *World Outside the Window: The Selected Essays.* Edited by Bradford Morrow. New York: New Directions, 1987. Rexroth's influence is pervasive, and his essays hard-hitting and scholarly. He can speak with conviction on alchemy, jazz, modern painting, Jewish mysticism, and anarchist politics. Particularly good essays on Japanese and Chinese poetry, Buddhist writers, and poets of the 1950s.

Scalapino, Leslie. *The Public World / Syntactically Impermanence.* Hanover, New Hampshire: Wesleyan University Press, 1999. Essays that grapple with contemporary strategies of poetry, and similarities between Zen thought and American writing. The focus stays on language itself, the expression of which is always "syntactically impermanence."

Schelling, Andrew. *The India Book: Essays and Translations from Indian Asia.* Oakland: O Books, 1993. Essays on Buddhist ecology, Sanskrit poetry, Tibetan song, classical Indian music, folklore, and other topics.

Schelling, Andrew. *Wild Form, Savage Grammar: Poetry, Ecology, Asia.* Albuquerque: La Alameda Press, 2003. Underlying threads of ecology, Buddhist teachings, and contemporary poetry weave through these essays, many of which investigate traditional Asian literature. Accounts of wolf reintroduction in the Rockies, Paleolithic cave art, early Indian poets, bioregionalism, etc.

Shirane, Harua. *Traces of Dreams: Landscape, Cultural Memory, and the Poetry of Basho.* Stanford, California: Stanford University Press, 1998. Fine study of Basho's various types of writing, his changes in style, and the poetry of the past that influenced him. One of the best books to go deep into haiku, haibun, and other Japanese forms of poetry.

Snyder, Gary. *Earth House Hold: Technical Notes & Queries to Fellow Dharma Revolutionaries.* New York: New Directions, 1969. Influential handbook for a Buddhist-anarchist-poetry counterculture. Includes several of Snyder's journals plus essays, reviews, manifestoes, translations of Zen literature, and an account of a sesshin at Daitoku-ji in Kyoto.

Snyder, Gary. *Passage Through India.* San Francisco: Grey Fox Press, 1983. Originally written as a letter to his sister Thea, this is Snyder's account of a half-year spent traveling in India—the same journey documented by Joanne Kyger in her *Strange Big Moon: Japan and India Journals* and by Allen Ginsberg.

Snyder, Gary. *The Practice of the Wild.* San Francisco: North Point Press, 1990. Explorations of language, nature, wilderness, and Buddhist practice. Snyder is the most subtle of contemporary thinkers on the place of wilderness in history, and the types of practice that permit the wild into one's daily existence.

Snyder, Gary. *The Real Work: Interviews & Talks* 1964–1979. New York: New Directions, 1980. Published after Snyder returned to North America (Turtle Island) from his nearly fifteen years in Japan studying Zen. Much of the thought here goes toward the practice of becoming native to North America: bioregionalism, family, appropriate technology, and Zen.

Stewart, Frank, ed. *The Poem Behind the Poem: Translating Asian Poetry.* Port Townsend: Copper Canyon, 2004. Accounts by contemporary translators of their relationship to the Asian traditions they work with—each essay a window into the poetry workshop, with side reminiscences of travel, friendships,

Buddhism and Taoism. Includes Snyder, Hamill, Hirshfield, Schelling, Sze, W.S. Merwin, and others.

Tarn, Nathaniel. *Views from the Weaving Mountain: Selected Essays in Poetics and Anthropology.* Albuquerque: University of New Mexico Press, 1991. Rigorous essays that include views of contemporary Buddhist thinkers, fellow poets, and Tarn's lifelong fieldwork as an anthropologist in Asia and Latin America.

Waldman, Anne and Andrew Schelling, eds. *Disembodied Poetics: Annals of The Jack Kerouac School.* Albuquerque: University of New Mexico Press, 1994. Naropa University (formerly The Naropa Institute) is the first Buddhist college in North America. Talks, lectures, and interviews by numerous resident and guest faculty of Naropa's Writing and Poetics Department. Includes Ginsberg, Whalen, Scalapino, Tarn, Snyder, along with Burroughs, Baraka, and others.

Weinberger, Eliot. *Works on Paper,* 1980–1986. New York: New Directions, 1986. Also see from the same publisher *Outside Stories* (1992) and *Karmic Traces* (2000). Weinberger is one of America's most cosmopolitan writers, equally at home in Asia, Latin America, or New York City. His essays have a dry, biting humor; mystical inclinations; curiosity about arcane matters; and an unswerving devotion to poetry as a spiritual path.

Whalen, Philip. *Off the Wall: Interviews with Philip Whalen.* Bolinas: Four Seasons, 1978. It would be hard to imagine anything more simple, authentic, and delightful than listening to Philip Whalen talk about poetry; his friendships with Kerouac, Snyder, Ginsberg, and others; and his curmudgeonly thoughts on Buddhist practice. This book needs to be expanded with Whalen's conversations and interviews of the eighties and nineties.

ABOUT WISDOM

Wisdom Publications, a nonprofit publisher, is dedicated to making available authentic Buddhist works for the benefit of all. We publish translations of the sutras and tantras, commentaries and teachings of past and contemporary Buddhist masters, and original works by the world's leading Buddhist scholars. We publish our titles with the appreciation of Buddhism as a living philosophy and with the special commitment to preserve and transmit important works from all the major Buddhist traditions.

To learn more about Wisdom, or to browse books online, visit our website at wisdompubs.org. You may request a copy of our mail-order catalog online or by writing to:

Wisdom Publications
199 Elm Street
Somerville, Massachusetts 02144 USA
Telephone: (617) 776-7416
Fax: (617) 776-7841
Email: info@wisdompubs.org
www.wisdompubs.org

THE WISDOM TRUST

As a nonprofit publisher, Wisdom is dedicated to the publication of fine Dharma books for the benefit of all sentient beings and dependent upon the kindness and generosity of sponsors in order to do so. If you would like to make a donation to Wisdom, please do so through our Somerville office. If you would like to sponsor the publication of a book, please write or email us at the address above.

Thank you.

Wisdom is a nonprofit, charitable 501(c)(3) organization affiliated with the Foundation for the Preservation of the Mahayana Tradition (FPMT).